D1186700

GRAND PRIX YEAR

GRAND PRIX YEAR

DAMON
HILL

THE INSIDE STORY OF A FORMULA ONE SEASON

PHOTOGRAPHS BY JON NICHOLSON

MACMILLAN

LIST OF CONTENTS

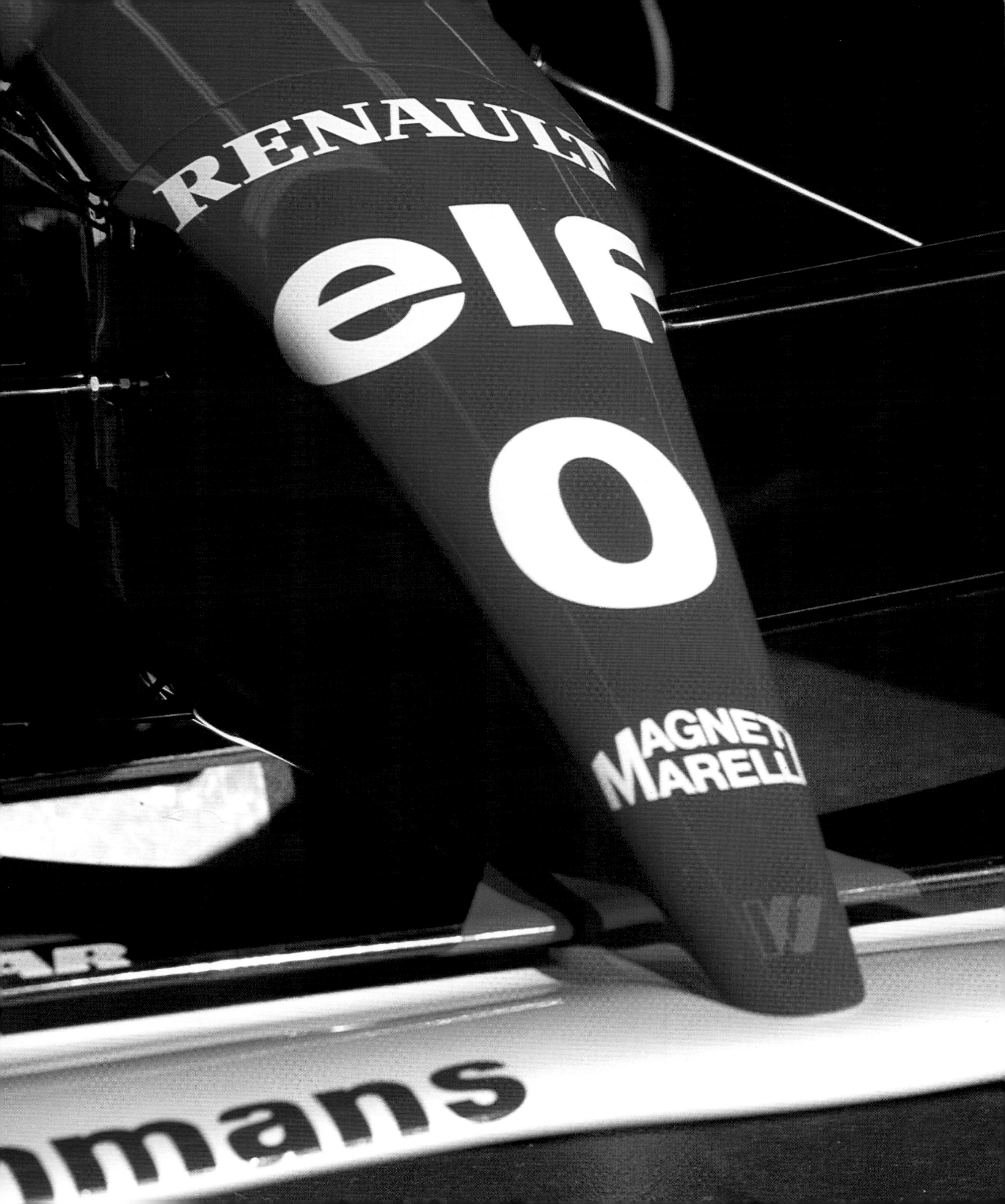
RENAULT
elf
0
MAGNETI
MARELLI

From the moment I signed for the Williams Grand Prix team in December 1992, I was catapulted from the cosy security of modest recognition into the fiercest spotlight of one of the world's most unforgiving sports. During the 1993 season I had to learn — and learn fast. Everything was new to me, the travel, the circuits, dealing with sponsor requests and the press; even some of the countries were unfamiliar. I barely had time to think, let alone write a book. So, I decided I really ought to record my second season and all the things which I found fascinating first time around, before I lost that sense of amazement, shock and surprise which I will surely do with the familiarity of routine.

To help me capture the drama, I took sports photographer Jon Nicholson with me everywhere I went. Jon is not only an excellent photographer, he is also a close friend. Therefore, the pictures in this book show me 'off duty' as well as presenting a 'professional front'. Jon also had access to places nobody should be allowed to go — and remembered his camera!

However, nobody could have predicted the terrible events that shocked the world when Austrian driver Roland Ratzenberger and then my team-mate Ayrton Senna were both killed in the same weekend. It is with much regret that this, my book, should have to carry the story of that terrible time, but we cannot pretend it never happened, just as we cannot forget that the season had moments of excitement and triumph.

It is my hope that this book should give an honest insight into the real world of Formula One.

DH, December 1994

CHAPTER ONE
EARLY DAYS

must have been the envy of thousands of motor racing fans. Born in 1960, I grew up in arguably one of the best eras of Grand Prix racing. Names such as Stirling Moss, Jim Clark, John Surtees, Jackie Stewart and my father, Graham Hill, were not only at the forefront of British sport, they were also winning races regularly and dominating the championship. And I was in the middle of it all.

I share the same birthday – 17 September – with Stirling Moss and, although his career had come to a premature end in 1962, he was very much a part of the motor racing scene, and still is. I can remember having pictures taken of Jim Clark and Stirling pushing me around the garden in a pedal car. I used to go to a number of the races, particularly the British Grand Prix, so I enjoyed a highly privileged position, one which young Formula One fans watching on the sidelines must have coveted like mad.

I didn't like being fussed over myself and, in any case, I wasn't really interested in motor racing

But the truth was, I didn't really have any interest in it at all. I simply took it as read that this was the way things were; it was perfectly normal and just as boring as anything else involving adults. I was amused by the activity surrounding my father; all the fuss and the way people reacted. But I wasn't particularly keen on the fact that so many people were clamouring for his attention. I didn't like being fussed over myself and, in any case, I wasn't really interested in motor racing.

I think it's a bit much to expect a five- or six-year-old boy to stand and watch a Grand Prix and, of course, in those days, the races weren't televised, so I never got the chance to fully appreciate what was going on. The fact is that I never really saw my father race. I can remember watching him win the 1969 Monaco Grand Prix because that, for some reason, was on television. I was playing in the garden and someone said, 'Come and watch your father win the race.' I only watched the last bit as he crossed the line; I was more interested in getting back to playing my game. It was almost a case of, 'He's won a race; so what?'

I never knew too much about exactly what my father did although, in our house, it was impossible to escape the fact that he was in motor racing; there were trophies, photographs and paintings all over the place. I remember when he won the Indianapolis 500 in 1966, there was a big party at the house and a huge sign outside

welcoming him home from America. I didn't know what it was all about. But I knew it was a big deal because everyone was so excited.

At the time, we were living in Mill Hill, in north-west London. Dad had a tiny office in that house but, when we moved to Lyndhurst in Hertfordshire in 1970, there was room for him to spread himself out. My bedroom was above his office, so I could hear him on the phone. I knew when he was there and I used to go into the office and spend a long time listening to him – you could never get the chance to actually talk to him.

It was a fascinating room. The walls were covered with BRDC (British Racing Drivers' Club) Gold Stars and there were all sorts of artefacts, including one of Richard Nixon's golf balls. He had met the US President at some stage and he always made a joke about having one of Nixon's balls. There were bottles of champagne and lots of the bits and bobs people give you. Again, there were pictures everywhere; Dad playing golf with Tony Jacklin; Dad getting up to all sorts of tricks such as dancing on a

I FELT AS UNCOMFORTABLE AS I LOOKED DOING THIS PUBLICITY SHOT FOR GOD KNOWS WHAT WITH MY FATHER AT ELSTREE AERODROME IN ABOUT 1970

I'M AFRAID I AM THE ONE WITH
THE DODGY SANDALS

table with no trousers on – that sort of thing. It really was a fantastic place to go into and just browse around. But, at that age, it is difficult to work out quite what you should think of it all.

All everyone talks to you about is your father and what he's getting up to. It seemed, too, that motor racing and his activities were all he talked about although that was not strictly true because he was very interested in a lot of other things. But if, say, we were to have people round for Sunday lunch then, naturally, my father and his racing would form 50 per cent of the conversation. I could never see the attraction in that.

I could never understand why these people were so interested in my father because, to me, he wasn't the extraordinary person he was to everyone else. The reason, of course, was that I didn't really know what he had done. I only realized the full extent of his achievements much later on and I then became a firm fan of Graham Hill.

But, in my youth, I just accepted that he did everything brilliantly and part of that was being a great racing driver. I never got worked up about it like a racing fan would have done. It meant I was pretty blasé about Formula One and I had no urge to be a racing driver. People expected me to follow in my father's footsteps – and I didn't want to do what was expected. In truth, I didn't really know what to expect of myself.

Motor bikes were the last thing on my mind. I had no concept of what they were about until, one day at Silverstone when I was eleven, I came across a Honda monkey bike in the paddock. I was given a go and I immediately knew what I wanted to do; I wanted to ride a bike, just like that one.

I pestered my Dad to the point where I found an advertisement for the same bike in a motor cycle magazine and pointed it out with poorly concealed longing, saying, 'I'd really like one of those.'

Not long after, Dad was racing at Brands Hatch and we were staying nearby, at our cottage in Kent. He asked me if I wanted to go with him to the races – which was very unusual – and I said I'd rather stay at home and play in the garden. Finally, he persuaded me to go. When we got there, he presented me with a Honda monkey bike. I was totally stunned. However, I was also very embarrassed that he had done it in front of an audience; everyone was there to see me get this thing. I felt awkward because there was always a fuss about everything associated with him – and now I was part of it.

And yet, I couldn't believe it. There was this motor bike, the one I had wanted. I've still got it, in fact, although it is a bit of a wreck now after someone crashed into the garage where it was being stored in Wandsworth.

When Dad got a Bultaco off-road bike, he let me have a go on it. It was bigger and more powerful and that was the start of it. I became totally fascinated with bikes, really stupid about them. I followed Evil Knievel and took an interest in anything to do with bikes; I had pictures covering my walls.

FORTUNATELY MY FATHER
LOVED BIKES TOO

It is hard to tell whether I was getting into bikes because they really appealed to me or because I wanted to do something different. I think it was positively led. I actually liked motor bikes and saw them as being much more exciting than cars.

At the time, Formula One was perhaps a bit too subtle for me. And, I have to say that, in the early 1970s, the Formula One cars were not particularly attractive. The cars from a decade before were great; they looked really nice. But then they went through an ugly phase and if you stood a motor bike alongside the 'lobster claw' Brabham which my Dad raced in 1971 then, to my mind, there was no comparison.

On top of that, the races were very long and usually very boring. I can remember Jackie Stewart going past the pits at Monza in Italy and then there would be a long

'APPREHENSIVE' COULD BE
A GOOD DESCRIPTION OF MY
MOTHER'S EXPRESSION HERE.
DESPITE THE OVERALLS I HAD
LITTLE INTEREST IN
MOTOR RACING

gap before another car appeared. And this would go on for two hours. It was the same at Silverstone in 1971; Jackie led from start to finish in perhaps the most tedious British Grand Prix of all time. So, all of that did little to raise my enthusiasm for motor racing.

I had discovered, however, that there was circuit racing for bikes and, naturally, I was attracted to it. Obviously it was a risky business and, after my father died in 1975, I was very reluctant to bring up the subject with my mother. But the compulsion was there. The opportunity arose to enter my road bike for a club race. I sawed the side-stand off the bike, went down to Lydden Hill in Kent, slept in a tent and had my first bike race. Then, like so many others, I realized that road bikes are no good on a track, so I wanted to get my hands on a race bike. That was the start of it.

I didn't do very well to begin with because I failed to appreciate that you need people to help you. I used to do everything myself. I assumed that, if I was going to be any good, then I'd win, no matter what I was on. If I was on a 250 cc machine and everyone else was on a 500 cc, then if I was any good, I'd win. I would get very frustrated and didn't realize soon enough that the preparation of the machine is really important. I used to think you simply jumped on the bike, went like stink – and became Barry Sheene. I really had my head in the clouds.

For instance, in the belief that a big rear tyre would mean more grip, I would fit the largest tyre I could find even though it was far too big for the rim. It never occurred to me that simply making sure you have the right tyre is so important. And I could never start the bike most of the time, so I'd be last off the grid. I was doing it completely blind and refusing any help. No one I knew went bike racing and I was either too stupid or too proud to ask anyone else. I just blundered on, banging my head against a brick wall.

A turning point came at Oulton Park. I had to change a tyre for some reason — probably a puncture — and as I struggled with the tyre levers at the back of the van, the rest of the field was going to the grid. I was wrestling with this thing, trying to get the tyre back on; it was a major flap.

I eventually reached the grid long after the rest had started. I was so fired up. It was all a blur until I suddenly found myself lying second to the guy who had been doing most of the winning. I was so startled I asked myself what on earth I was

I suddenly realized that there were other elements to this business; it was all about state of mind and being prepared

doing. Something clicked at that moment. I suddenly realized that there were other elements to this business; it was all about state of mind and being prepared. It was obvious that I needed help.

I was twenty-one at the time and was a dispatch rider during the week. They might send me on a Friday evening to somewhere like Walsall and I would get back at about midnight. Then I'd prepare the bike and head for the race track at perhaps three in the morning. You had no chance operating like that. Eventually, you think, 'I'm not going to carry on like this; it's not getting me anywhere.'

The following year, I didn't have enough money to race properly so I bought a bike from a friend and recognized that I would have to go back a step or two and tackle it at a level I could maintain. I was restricted to racing at Brands Hatch rather than travelling far and wide, because that was all I could afford. I had someone tune the bike properly and fit some decent carburettors. I concentrated solely on doing it right.

Brands Hatch was only forty minutes from where I lived, which meant I could get some sleep the night before and arrive at the circuit reasonably refreshed. I won everything in sight. No one beat me. It was brilliant.

Tackling some of the corners on the long circuit at Brands was an incredible experience. There was a bump on the inside of Westfield bend; you had to get off the seat for that one, let the bike go and then get back on the power as soon as possible.

The plunge down the hill and up the other side to the quick right-hander at

PEOPLE TELL <u>ME</u> TO LOOK HAPPY!

YOU CAN SEE WHERE I GET

IT FROM

GRAND PRIX YEAR

Hawthorn was fantastic. On one occasion, a pump came off and sprayed oil all over the back wheel, just as I got to Hawthorn. The bike went on its side and threw me half over the handle bars. I did a bit of a tank-slapper, the bike thrashing around as we went off the road at the exit of the corner and headed

At first I thought the cars were pretty horrible-looking things but, once in the cockpit, I forgot all that because they were quite good fun to drive

towards the woods. Somehow I managed to coax it back and we went all the way between Hawthorn and Westfield on the grass. I don't know how I stayed on. My heart was really thumping. It wasn't nice; not at all, but the track marshals appreciated the show!

Racing bikes may be incredibly dangerous but I had great fun doing it. I would love to go back and have another go, but I daren't. I won't allow myself that pleasure because a broken collarbone or a broken arm means I would miss too much of the Grand Prix season. It's a small price to pay considering where I am now.

I don't think my mother was too keen on me racing bikes and, for my part, I had begun to realize that very few people get to make a good career out of it. But I still had this feeling that I wanted to be in some form of motor sport.

My mother had met Mike Knight from the Winfield racing drivers' school in France and he suggested that I should try a course. He was keen for the school to find a British winner and, obviously, he realized that he could earn a bit of mileage from any association with the Hill name. My Mum preferred the idea of four wheels instead of two and it was suggested that I give the school a try to see if I liked it. I said that I would do it – but I couldn't afford to pay because all of my money, such as it was, went on the bike. When she offered to pay, I accepted because I could see this as a week in France and a bit of a laugh. That was the way I approached it.

To my astonishment, I quite enjoyed the course and did rather well. At first I thought the cars were pretty horrible-looking things but, once in the cockpit, I forgot all that because they were quite good fun to drive. And the thought also occurred that racing drivers, unlike bike riders, don't seem to spend their lives in hospital. Even though I had managed to avoid serious injury, there is no doubt that was a factor in persuading me to make the switch.

John Webb, the brains behind Brands Hatch at the time, helped get me my first race. He could see a PR opportunity for his circuit and, typically, I jumped in at the deep end. I reckoned I knew Brands Hatch but, of course, it was very different in a car. I simply did not know what I was doing.

Webb, meanwhile, had been working overtime and, on the day, the media was there in force, including a film crew from News at Ten. I was all over the papers but the story was not brilliant from my point of view. The car – a Formula Ford 2000 – was very difficult to drive and I spun off. Having learned my lesson on bikes, I quickly realized that I really ought to start at the beginning. I needed to step back and spend a season racing in Formula Ford with cars which were less powerful and not quite as sophisticated as the FF 2000.

I spent 1984 looking for a budget and, eventually, I got sponsorship from the Ricoh photocopying company. This meant I could do the last part of the season. I finished fifth in the Formula Ford Festival – a major end-of-term event – and received an award for 'best newcomer', which probably helped me find the money to do a full season in 1985.

Now I was taking motor racing very seriously. I was starting to win races and already I was thinking of Formula One. But there was the pressure of knowing I had started late compared with everyone else.

The accepted path was to move from Formula Ford into Formula Ford 2000 and then on to Formula Three. I decided to bypass 2000 and miss out a stage by going straight to Formula Three. It was a risk which didn't really pay off because I was to spend three years in Formula Three. It's a formula where you need a good budget – and I didn't have one. Occasionally, I managed a decent result; I came second once, I remember. But I also crashed quite a bit . . .

Paying to have the privilege of driving and racing someone's car is very common all the way through the sport

Nonetheless, I had showed enough promise to land a drive with the Cellnet team. The 1987 season started off with an Italian by the name of Massimo Monti, but he was unhappy living in England and was soon replaced with Martin Donnelly. That perked me up, because Martin was very fast. He was highly rated and I knew it would be good for me to have him in the team – rather like 1993 and 1994 in Formula One; you raise your game to match your team-mate. Donnelly kept the pressure on me and I learned a great deal racing against him; it was valuable experience.

In my third season, I won the supporting race for the British Grand Prix, a high profile occasion and a great place to pull off a victory. I felt on top of the world. Eddie Jordan asked if I wanted to take a drive he had available in his Formula 3000 team and, since this was one step away from Grand Prix racing, I didn't need to be asked twice.

Then he said, 'Fine, it'll be £70,000,' and, in my naiveté, I said, 'But wait a minute, you've just offered me the drive.' I was so taken aback, I didn't work out that what you needed to do was agree and then find a way of paying later. I think that's what Martin did when Jordan offered him the drive. I had the impression that he had put everything on the line financially and rumour suggested he had also signed a management contract with Jordan himself to get the drive which was, at the time, a good career move even if it was a questionable thing to do financially. Paying to have the privilege of driving and racing someone's car is very common all the way through the sport; it's simply a matter of priorities and how far you wish to extend yourself.

I had already taken a big gamble with Formula Three in 1986 and I didn't want to do it again. I was not in favour of promising to pay money I didn't have and end up in a deep hole as a result. I felt cheated over the Jordan drive because it seemed to me that I had been offered it first. After the high of winning at Silverstone, the rest of the 1988 season was miserable. There I was, stuck in Formula Three and my team-mate was racing in Formula 3000. I was demoralized by that

The following year started off no better; I had no drive, not even the promise of one. Absolutely nothing came up and I didn't know what I was going to do. Things were looking bleak financially, because there was no money coming in. I'd got married in 1988, we'd just bought a house and my wife, Georgie, had to give up work following the birth of our first boy, Oliver, who had Downs' Syndrome. There was no alternative but to try a different tack, which was to simply drive for money.

I remember going to watch the Formula 3000 race at Silverstone, early in the season. Colin Bennett, one of the entrants, asked me if I wanted a drive. My immediate reaction was to enquire how much money he wanted. When he said it wouldn't cost me a thing, I found it hard to believe. This was a small team, about to start running in the British Formula 3000 series. Obviously, this was a domestic championship and nothing like as important as the European series which Jordan had been talking about earlier on, but I reckoned it was better than doing nothing at all.

Things were looking bleak financially, because there was no money coming in

As well as doing a bit in the British Touring Car Championship (and getting paid for it) I was also asked to share a Porsche at Le Mans. That was an incredible experience. Apart from three lengths of a runaway at Le Mans airport, my first brief run in the car was during practice, at dusk. The Porsche 962 was doing 220 mph on the Mulsanne Straight and the next time I drove the car was in the race itself!

I loved it. I thought it was one of the most exciting things I had ever done; driving at night, going round and round, watching the dials, just trying to do the job. At the end of the first stint, I couldn't get out of the car. It was so hot inside and I had a screaming headache. I thought, 'What have I let myself in for?' It was horrible. But, after that, I settled in and started doing double stints at night. It was great even though the skin was coming off my hand, thanks to the gear change being so stiff; you really had to push it in. It was good fun – but frightening too. Sitting there at 220 mph for over a minute on a straight, it was easy to start thinking, 'Well, I just hope a wheel doesn't fall off!'

It was valuable experience because all they wanted was for me to do the job right; no heroics or anything like that. It was far removed from driving a Formula One car and yet this was just the sort of attitude needed when I started testing for Williams a few years later.

It was a strange year, 1989, because the next offer came from the Japanese Footwork team. It was international Formula 3000 and it was a paid drive. But it was a car which nobody wanted; it was thought to be so bad that the Footwork was considered to be the kiss of death as far as your career was concerned. I thought,

'Well, I need the money. I'll take it.' My attitude was that if I could drive the wheels off this thing and do better than anyone expected, then there was a chance of something else arising from the drive. Besides, it would be useful experience in Formula 3000; more mileage under my belt.

Right enough, the car wasn't particularly good. In fact, I thought it was dreadful. I was completely restricted by the physical limit of what the car would do but I qualified for every race — something of a novelty for the team — and usually finished dead last. At Spa-Francorchamps, a fantastic road circuit in Belgium, I qualified reasonably well. That made people sit up and take notice. They began to ask what I could do with a good car if I could manage to go that well in the Footwork. And that led to a drive in a Lola, which was a good car.

People began to ask what I could do with a good car

In 1990, I led over fifty per cent of the races, had three consecutive pole positions, started most of them from the front row but never won a single race. Some mechanical gremlin would always lead to a retirement. To say it was frustrating hardly makes a start when describing what I and the Middlebridge team suffered that year. But I had shown my mettle and that was enough to convince Williams that I should get the job as test driver. It was probably the turning point of my career.

In 1991, the latest — and not as good as its predecessor — Lola was beaten hands down by everything else in the Formula 3000 field. I was the only person who managed to lead a race in a Lola that year but, really, we were fighting it all the way; it was hopeless.

Although I had a testing contract with Williams, I knew I just had to get out of Formula 3000 after nearly three seasons. The team I had driven for in Formula 3000 also owned the Brabham Grand Prix team, so I knew the people running the Formula One cars. Again, it wasn't the best of cars but when the chance arose to drive one in the 1992 Spanish Grand Prix, I thought, 'Well, I've got to race something.'

I failed to qualify for that race and the rest of the season was a struggle, although I did manage to get into the races in Britain and Hungary. I was in the slightly bizarre situation of testing for the best team and recording lap times which were quicker than those being achieved by the likes of Ayrton Senna in a McLaren. And then I would go to the same circuit for the Grand Prix proper and end up at the back of the grid in the Brabham. I'd sit and watch Nigel Mansell take off from pole position and I knew that I could do better for myself if I was in that car. But I didn't really believe there was much chance of getting a Grand Prix drive with Williams.

Then Nigel moved out of Formula One and Riccardo Patrese, his team-mate, moved on to Benetton. Williams signed Alain Prost – which left one vacant seat. I kept my head down when I was testing the car and I kept pestering Frank Williams when I was out of it. Eventually, he could bear it no longer and decided I had done enough to convince them of my potential. Damon Hill became a Grand Prix driver with Williams-Renault. My life was about to change beyond all recognition.

My approach to 1993 was one of keeping my head down. And yet, from the word go, there were people trying to make a story out of it

1993 was a completely new experience for me with regard to the amount of attention I was receiving as a driver. I had been slotted into the vacuum left by Nigel – the reigning world champion – who was leaving at the height of his Formula One career. He was driving very well and he was very newsworthy in many ways.

I didn't want to be newsworthy. I just wanted to be able to do my job because I knew it would be difficult enough doing that. I didn't want to have to cope with any controversy at all. My approach to 1993 was one of keeping my head down. And yet, from the word go, there were people trying to make a story out of it. It is all very well having a lot of media attention, but you have got to back it up with results.

I was very keen to make sure I got some decent finishes as soon as possible while, at the same time, not making any mistakes. There was a lot of pressure on that side because I knew that Renault and, to some degree, Frank Williams, would be watching closely to see how this experiment would turn out. And it was an experiment of sorts because they had taken the test driver and made him the race driver in a top team, one which was accustomed to consistent success. I had a great deal of support from the team; that was important to me. But I knew that support would only last for as long as I was doing the job in the car. In Formula One, there is no room for self-induce failure.

The problem was, I didn't really know what I was preparing myself for because I had never done it before. The demands made upon a Grand Prix driver away from the race track have to be experienced to be believed. Your head is filled with so many things to think about and 1993 was a lesson in discovering what it is reasonably possible to achieve while being a Grand Prix driver at the same time. If your mind is a muscle, then in 1993 I had to think like Arnold Schwarzenegger.

I had to learn to come to terms with the fact that I was not going to be left alone by the media. Suddenly I was faced with people I didn't know looking at me all the time and watching what I was doing. I found that very uncomfortable — even to the point where I felt awkward when I mounted the podium after winning my first Grand Prix. I didn't really know the procedure. I knew what to do as far as driving the car was concerned, but I hadn't really thought about what the form should be on the rostrum. So, I did what a normal embarrassed person does; I bowed!

That win in Hungary was the first of three on the trot, and they went a long way towards proving my case for being in the team in the first place. Now I could claim to have done something useful. I didn't feel quite so vulnerable because now I could say, 'I've been successful. I've won a Grand Prix.'

Nonetheless, I didn't think I had shown precisely what I was capable of in 1993. I felt for the most part of the season that I could drive better — but I couldn't afford to take the risk. I believed there was more to come. And that was the perfect way to go into 1994.

CHAPTER TWO

TESTING

PRIVATE FREEDOM: ENJOYING
PRE-SEASON HOLS IN ANTIGUA
WITH OLIVER AND JOSHUA

Although the actual racing did not start until the end of March, we were hard at work throughout the winter. Or most of it, anyway. I managed to get away with Georgie, Oliver and Joshua for two weeks when we went to Antigua just after Christmas. But a fortnight was not really enough; I could have done with another month. Having time together like that was invaluable, something to keep me going through the next eleven months.

It was back to business immediately on our return and I suppose you could say that the new season was formally kicked off with a major press launch at Estoril in Portugal. Williams had a change of sponsor, Rothmans International introducing them-

CLOSE CROP CLOSE-UP. INSPECTING MY '94 HAIRCUT IN THE MIRRORS. ROTHMANS' LAUNCH, ESTORIL

selves with a well-organized two-day affair which gave 400 journalists the opportunity to see my new team-mate and I parade in our Rothmans overalls for the first time.

Ayrton Senna had replaced Alain Prost and, naturally, everyone was speculating over how we would get on – and who would be the quickest. It is impossible to answer questions like that at such an early stage. There was so much to do and I was simply straining at the leash, keen to get my hands on a car.

There had been time to organize my side of things; now I wanted to do some testing, really get down to it. There may have been two months between then and the first race but I knew as well as anyone that the time would simply fly by, particularly after the new car first appeared in February.

In theory, each new car is so well thought out that it should work straight away. But you need to prove that the car is going to be safe enough and fast enough – and that means constantly trying to improve the product. That's what testing is all about and it reaches an intense level as time starts to run out.

Being a racing driver is not simply about going quickly in the races. The measure of a good driver is closely linked to how capable he is of telling the designers and engineers what he is feeling from the performance of the car. There have been many examples of top drivers being able to detect a problem on the car before it was actually noticeable from the outside. People like Jackie Stewart, for instance, could come into the pits, saying the car felt strange. The mechanics would check the car over and eventually discover that the suspension was on the point of failure. He had managed to feel it but there was no way they would have spotted the problem without being pointed in the right direction.

During testing, you have to be alert to all the changing sensations and experiences that the car is giving you throughout the day or the week of testing. Then you refer that to the catalogue of experiences you have had during your career with different cars, or indeed, with the same car but in different circumstances.

These are memories and sensations; nothing more than that. They can't be measured by computer; they are not recordable. Even though the cars these days are loaded with computers, they cannot produce the measurements and graph curves which would, in effect, say 'this is going to be the best car you've ever driven because it says so on the computer'. You still need to put the driver in the car and see what he can do with it; ask him whether he thinks the car is any good or not.

The measure of a good driver is closely linked to how capable he is of telling the designers and engineers what he is feeling from the performance of the car

When I first started testing for Williams, I had the idea that, somehow, I would be told what to do. I would then drive the car round and round, bring it back in and they would check the data. But it soon became apparent that what I had to say was regarded as valuable information, no matter how I might consider it.

The years of experience accumulated by people such as Patrick Head, director of design and engineering at Williams, and Adrian Newey, chief designer, meant that any suspicion of a feeling about the car could be cross-referenced mentally and compared with drivers' comments going back a decade or more. The most seemingly insignificant remarks could hold a key to improving the car's performance or rectifying a potential problem.

Testing can be extremely demanding; more so than racing. The only difference is, you are not racing in close proximity to anyone else; you are free to do what you like on the race track. The circuit is often hired by the team, or a number of teams, for their exclusive use for perhaps a week. During that time, you may do simulated endurance runs and Grand Prix distances, just to see if the car has any mechanical weaknesses. It's all very well having a car that is super-quick over a given lap but it is no good to you if unreliability is going to be a constant problem.

I came to appreciate that if a refinement on the car was not usable in a Grand Prix, then it would be of no use to me or anyone else

When I was working for Williams, purely as a test driver, it was made plain to me from the start that I was not there to set new lap records. Nor had I been given the best car in Formula One purely for my own personal pleasure.

It was not necessary to drive the car flat out anyway because that would not be much use to anyone if it could only be kept up for five laps. A good day's testing can be anything up to 70 laps, or even 100 on a good day – nearly two complete Grand Prix distances! So, my job was to drive at a pace, probably at around 95 per cent of the car's potential, which would allow the engineers to do their respective jobs.

Along the way, I was becoming familiar with how the team worked and the technical aspects of it all, as well as learning the circuits and the physical requirements of driving a Formula One car very quickly. I felt at the end of the first year as test driver that I could get in a Formula One car and give it some stick – and that's not something you can do straight away, regardless of how good you are.

My priorities were affected by the change in 1993 from being solely a test driver to going racing as well. In my first year with Williams, I was interested only in the performance of the car. But, after a season of racing, I came to appreciate that if a refinement on the car was not usable in a Grand Prix, then it would be of no use to me or anyone else.

Previously, if it had improved the lap time, then that was the ultimate criterion, regardless of whether or not it was a practical development for use in a 200-mile race. I have since learned how to gather the information gleaned from testing and apply it to what I would need at a Grand Prix; the two things are often quite different.

Testing is a nine-to-five job in the sense that you get up quite early and try to cram as much food in your mouth before the nine a.m. start. You need a considerable amount of energy because, as I have already mentioned, quite often you will cover

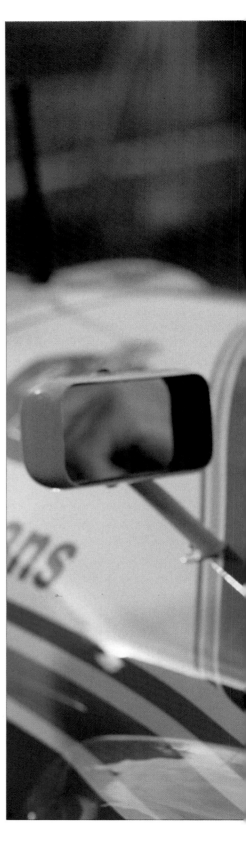

more miles in a day's testing than you would in a Grand Prix.

By the fifth day, you can be pretty exhausted and drained. After four days of solid running, you climb into the car at nine o'clock on the Friday morning and, as soon as you go through the first corner, you are aware of the battering your body has been subjected to. You've got bruises on your knees, elbows and knuckles. And you can actually hear your neck cracking.

Obviously, you do your best to make the car as comfortable as possible – certainly, that's very important for a Grand Prix distance – but it's impossible to get away with constantly subjecting yourself to the G-forces and speeds involved without your body suffering in some way. The driver is tested just as much as the car on these occasions.

In many ways, testing is similar to practising for any other sport. But the difference is that a golfer might practise his swing five or six days a week, whereas the Grand Prix driver only has that opportunity maybe three or four times every month; sometimes, during the winter, it may not be as often as that. So, testing is the only chance a driver gets to hone his skills with the machine he will be using in the competition itself. Track time is limited because it costs a lot of money to run a Formula One car and, of course, there are only so many places where you can do it.

You learn to utilize to the maximum whatever track time you have available. It is necessary to polish your driving while discovering more about the car. This is the time to try different rollbars and brake pads, change the engine mapping, learn

ETHEREAL COLLABORATION: CHASSIS MEETS ENGINE. BERNARD DUDOT (RENAULT) APPEARS SPECTRE-LIKE BEFORE PATRICK HEAD (WILLIAMS) AT THE RICARD TEST

'IT'S . . . ER . . . WHAT'SNAME.'
FAILING A SIMPLE POP QUIZ ON
CAPITAL RADIO AGAINST AN
AUDIENCE WHICH WAS VASTLY
BETTER PREPARED

about the effects of subtle changes such as leaning the air-fuel mixture or richening it. You have to assimilate all of that while doing a number of laps and, at the same time, producing a competitive lap time.

There's a lot going on and it can be extremely demanding, not only for the driver, but for everyone else on the team. You need caterers at the track to feed the army of personnel, particularly the mechanics who often find themselves working from seven thirty a.m. until perhaps two the following morning. After three or four days of that, they are wiped out and the first thing the driver must remember each day is to thank his mechanics for getting the car back together, ready for another day's work. The mechanics deserve appreciation because they have to work at a relentless pace; in the winter, the garages are freezing and conditions are far from perfect.

The engineers, who are calculating the changes and their effects all the time, feel that their brains are frazzled by Friday evening. But the nature of the game is such that, despite the hardship, you find yourself saying at the end of the week: 'Right, can we leave here knowing we have found a set-up which will work at the next race? Am I happy with the car? What can I do to improve it?'

No matter how hard you try during testing, it's not quite the same as the actual racing. The buzz is missing

The problem is that, no matter how hard you try during testing, it's not quite the same as the actual racing. The buzz is missing. You put everything into a quick lap during testing but the adrenalin does not get pumped up like it does during qualifying. So, when you sit down afterwards and ask yourself, 'Where can we go quicker?' it is a very difficult question to answer. Sometimes it's hard to know whether the car could be improved or whether it's your driving that needs looking at.

If there is a deficiency in the car, you can overcome that by adapting your driving style to get round the problem. But that's not the answer in the long term because the only way the car is going to go quicker is by making it better, not by side-stepping the problem with your driving and then thinking everything is okay. It's true that a driver can only overcome so much by adapting his driving but, at the same time, he will be wary of making the car too easy to drive. When that happens, you begin to wonder if you are not going fast enough; you become suspicious of a car that is easy to drive.

I am often asked how it is possible to take a racing car close to its limit and yet, simultaneously, take note of what it is doing. The point is that to go really fast requires total concentration in itself. So, how can you also take time not only to observe and feel what is going on, but remember it later?

You become sensitive to the most ridiculously small changes in the car — but you have to be careful you are not imagining them

It's a bit like watching television and listening to what someone is telling you at the same time. If you can stay with the plot and also take on board what the person is saying, then that's what testing is like. You have to learn to open up your senses. You carry on as normal but, while driving the car, things which are different stand out. You become sensitive to the most ridiculously small changes in the car – but you have to be careful you are not imagining them. You are, in a way, open to all sorts of suggestions.

For instance, when we go tyre testing with Goodyear, they might bring along five different types of tyre, plus a set of control tyres which are a known quantity. They don't actually tell me what is being put on the car and it could be, if they felt mischievous, that the shuffling round of the tyres resulted in a set of control tyres each time. Because you are searching for any little detail changes, and your senses are so alert, it is possible that you could imagine things and come back each time reporting something different for each set, even though they are the same. That's a hypothetical example and, in any case, I'm pretty confident I could tell that the tyres are exactly the same. Or, at least, I had better be able to by now.

Tyre testing is a separate thing entirely to working on the car. When you are testing tyres, you don't change anything on the car because you want it to be constant throughout, otherwise the experiments with the tyres are invalid.

Generally speaking, the tyres can differ in two ways: the compound (the mixture of rubber which makes up the actual tread) and the method of construction. The aim is to get the right combination of both for a given circuit. For example, a particular construction on the front tyre could give you a positive feeling from the car; you could position it precisely going into a corner. On the other hand, the wrong construction might make the car feel unstable, almost as if it is going to fall over when going through a corner.

At the back of your mind there is always the thought that a driving error could result in the car being damaged

If all of this is done scientifically, then you will make progress. But, always, the tyre manufacturers are assuming that the driver is a constant factor in the testing process. And, while he is doing his best to be totally consistent, that is not always possible. You only have to look at golf to know that it is feasible to hit the ball brilliantly one day and yet, the next day, even though the player is doing exactly the same thing, he can't hit a thing — and there is no explanation for it. It's the same with driving. One day, the test driver might like the sensation of a soggy tyre and the next day he might hate it. The trick is to be as consistent and as honest as you can.

This underlines the huge responsibility resting on the shoulders of the test driver. People such as Renault have a massive investment in their engine development programme. It is the same with Elf fuel, and the brake people, the tyre companies and so on. Every time the car runs, there is a list of questions from all these divisions and they want answers.

What the driver says can have a major bearing on how the manufacturers of the various components react to the changes they have made to their product. Initially, I was afraid to open my mouth. I would say something like, 'Well, I think it's better. . .

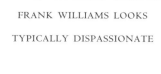

FRANK WILLIAMS LOOKS

TYPICALLY DISPASSIONATE

but don't go and make a completely different brake pad on my say-so.' That changed as I gained more confidence in my assessments. It can reach the point where, as you improve, you can sense with almost a hundred per cent certainty whether things are better or not.

Once you are at the track, you could be at any circuit in the world; they seem pretty much the same wherever you are

In addition to this, at the back of your mind there is always the thought that a driving error could result in the car being damaged. That could set the schedule back so badly that we might have to start from scratch again. And that could jeopardize the development programme which, in turn, could affect the remainder of the season. So, obviously, there is a lot of pressure, but people imagine there is a fair bit of romance attached to this. 'A week in Portugal in January? How nice!' That sort of thing.

When you go testing, you see nothing but the hotel and the circuit. Even though activity on the track may finish at five, or even six o'clock, you will be at the circuit until perhaps eight or nine. When you eventually return to the hotel, you simply want a hot bath and then you're ready to crash out. And I can tell you that Portugal in January is still pretty cold. It's still pitch black at ten to nine in the morning and dusk – well, there hardly seems to be any dusk; it is as if someone switched out the light at about six p.m.

But it is nice sometimes. When we are testing at Estoril, I try and take the coast

road to the circuit. It is the long way round but that can be your only moment of relaxation; certainly, it's the only chance you get to appreciate the scenery. Once you are at the track, you could be at any circuit in the world; they seem pretty much the same wherever you are.

You would think there is time to relax at the circuit, particularly when the car is being worked on and the driver is hanging around. But, the trouble is, you don't feel like relaxing. A good example of this occurred when I went to Spain for my first serious test of the winter. I hadn't driven for six weeks and I was really keen to get stuck in. I went past the pits for the first time, accelerating along the main straight. When I pushed the button to start changing down through the gears for the first corner, something went wrong in the gearbox and it threw me off the road and into the wall.

If you've done your job right, then most of the work for a race will have been done during testing

The accident destroyed the gearbox and the engine. Because of that, and other problems which had cropped up, it was a day and a half before I got to drive the car again. I spent all that time kicking my heels and wondering what I could do to help, thinking about what might improve the car. The answer was 'very little' because I hadn't got a car and I hadn't done any miles. So there was nothing I could contribute. It was a day and a half wasted as far as I was concerned, and that does little to relax you.

Even when things are going well, it is inevitable there will be mechanical failures from time to time; after all, that is one of the purposes of the test. So, you are waiting for the car to be repaired and, if you are tired, your mind goes off the job. You have to remind yourself constantly just why you are there. Inevitably, you end up having stupid conversations with the mechanics and team personnel, just to lighten the atmosphere. And you find yourself making endless cups of tea, eating too many biscuits and cranking up Frank Williams's bill by using the telephone laid on in the truck.

It can seem lonely occasionally although, increasingly, there will be various demands on your time; other things for you to do, such as interviews. I try to avoid interviews while testing. My belief is that it is necessary to concentrate more, comparatively speaking, during testing than it is during the two days of practice at a Grand Prix. If you've done your job right, then most of the work for a race will have been covered during testing. Testing, therefore, is the only time when we have the luxury of time itself.

CHAPTER THREE
THE
NEW CAR

THE BRAZILIAN GRAND PRIX

POSING TO PERFECTION.
THE PRE-SEASON WEIGH-IN GIVES
EVERYONE A CHANCE TO GET
THEIR MUG SHOTS

The beginning of the 1994 season saw the introduction of a new set of regulations for Formula One. The computer controlled suspension systems (active suspension) and 'traction control' devices, all of which contributed to making the job of driving the car much easier than it might otherwise have been, were banned, but we would now be permitted to refuel during a race.

These measures introduced a new set of parameters within which we had to work to extract the maximum potential from our driver/chassis/engine package. The rear tyres would now suffer more from the damage caused by excess wheel spin – previously controlled by the traction devices. The critical ride height of the car above the ground, which affects its very sensitive aerodynamics, could only ever be a compromise as we were no longer allowed to use the computer to optimize the 'ground effect'. In addition, thanks to the refuelling, the start weight of the cars could be reduced by running as little as a quarter of the previous season's starting fuel load, thus considerably increasing their speed.

The underlying reason for the changes was that it was felt that making the cars more difficult to drive might make the racing more interesting. The refuelling could also add a tactical element to further increase the excitement.

Whether or not this really would happen was impossible to say so early in the season. All it meant to me and to the rest of the Williams team was that we would effectively be starting from scratch and have to do a better job than all our rivals. So in that respect nothing much had changed – except one thing. All the hard work Williams and I had done to develop a state of the art car had been negated by the new rules and we had to start all over again.

The underlying reason for the technical changes was that it was felt that making the cars more difficult to drive might make the racing more interesting

When a racing driver talks about trying a new Formula One car for the first time, it conjures the sort of cosy image which comes with taking delivery of a new car from the showroom. People think of the smell of upholstery and carpets; the feel of machinery that is taut and precise; a ride that is smooth and free from the rattles and squeaks which come with wear and tear.

A racing driver does not view his new car that way. In fact, he usually thinks it's pretty horrible. Because everything is new, the joints will be stiff; controls such as the steering will feel heavy and cumbersome. You actually prefer getting into a racing car which has done a few miles and has loosened up.

But, the trouble is, the team is constantly changing everything. Once you get to a point where things have begun to feel free and more comfortable, the team will replace those parts and you go back to dealing with a car which suddenly feels stiff and less manageable again. A new Formula One car is far from 'nice' in the accepted sense of the motoring expression.

Driver comfort is very important, of course, but not in the air-conditioned, real leather, deep-pile carpet criteria associated with a road car. We're not talking about luxury and opulence but rather the fundamental need not to have any distractions caused by discomfort in the cockpit. If you find that the driving position in your road

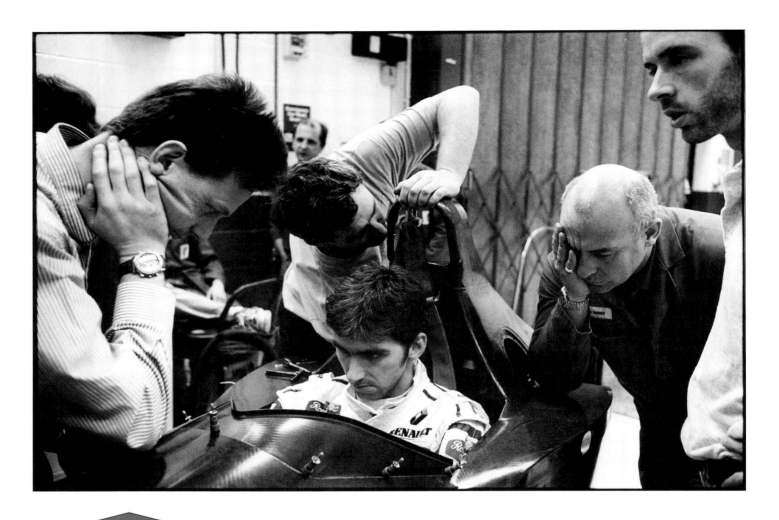

'SIX FEET TALL AND SIZE ELEVEN
FEET . . . NOW HE TELLS US!'
WILLIAMS ENGINEERS SQUEEZE A
QUART INTO A PINT POT

car needs altering, you can make small adjustments as you go along. If you begin to feel stiff or sore, there is always the opportunity to stop and do something about it.

In a Grand Prix car, you've made your bed and you must lie on it – so to speak. Once a race starts, you have to put up with what you've got. A niggling problem in such a harsh environment can quickly became a major source of pain which could affect your performance. That is why a massive amount of time is spent with a new car making sure that the cockpit fits the driver like a glove. The Brazilian Grand Prix may have been the first race on the calendar on 27 March but a huge amount of work had been done with the new car before we even thought about setting off for Sao Paulo.

When I go to the Williams factory to sit in a new car for the first time, my main concern is whether or not there will be enough room for me. That may sound a curious thing to say but, when you are six feet tall and possess size eleven feet, there is very little room for manoeuvre in every sense of the expression. The designers are always looking to trim down the car as much as possible in order to find whatever aerodynamic advantage they can and, if you are not careful, they will leave less and less room for the driver actually to do his job.

A massive amount of time is spent with a new car making sure that the cockpit fits the driver like a glove

The internal dimensions of the Williams-Renault FW16 were much the same as the 1993 car although, in certain areas, the cockpit was very much tighter. There was less room for switches, knobs and so on and it was simply a case of finding somewhere to put items such as the rollbar and brake balance adjusters.

Experience tells you what is right and what could cause a problem during a race. It is all very well saying that you can twiddle such and such a knob while sitting in the car at the factory. It's quite another thing to find the correct control while you're trying to drive one-handed up the hill at Monaco with the other hand bouncing all over the place.

You constantly have to apply knowledge accumulated over the years as you sit in the cockpit of a new car. A simple matter such as the positioning of the pedals is terribly important, particularly when you consider that the car is usually leaping about and your legs are being thrown around and yet you have to hit the brake pedal in exactly the right place every time. When you are slowing from 200 mph to 60 mph

Apart from when you pull out of the garage and after the start of the race, your left foot remains completely inactive

in less than two seconds, there is no time for two stabs at the pedal.

The fact is that most of the people who work on the car cannot actually get into the narrow cockpit. When you throw your legs forward and put your knees together, there is about an inch to spare either side of your knees and probably even less at your feet. And yet, despite those restrictions, you have got to be able to operate the pedals and move without getting cramp. Apart from when you pull out of the garage and after the start of the race, your left foot remains completely inactive. It stays on the foot rest and acts as a means of bracing yourself. It is the right leg which does all the work.

Pressing the brake pedal requires a lot of strength. You have only a split second in which to move your foot from the throttle to the brake and you do it not by pivoting on your heel, but by lifting your foot and pushing your leg forward. It is like doing leg presses and the crucial thing is being able to feel the pedal. That is why it is important to hit the pedal in exactly the same place every time because you want to have the same sensation each time you brake.

The track at Montreal, for example, calls for a lot of braking on every lap and, during the 1993 Canadian Grand Prix, I had a particularly hard brake pedal. After about twenty laps, my foot went numb. I was pressing the pedal so hard that I had managed to cut the circulation; I couldn't feel my foot on either the throttle or the brake. For about a week afterwards, I had a burning sensation in my foot and I was worried that I might have damaged a nerve.

After an experience like that, I worked hard on developing a driving boot which had the right amount of stiffness in the sole and yet was supple enough elsewhere not to create a lot of pressure on any part of my foot.

On first acquaintance with the new car, you climb into the cockpit and sit on a bin liner which is filled with quick-setting foam

Most important of all is the seat and we take a great deal of time and care over that. On first acquaintance with the new car, you climb into the cockpit and sit on a bin liner which is filled with quick-setting foam. Once you have found as near to an ideal driving position as you can, the foam expands around you. It's quite a pleasant sensation because the foam is really warm; it's like having a hot bath. But, because the foam is so powerful, it can force you into positions you don't really want to be in and it's quite a tricky operation to get the mould exactly as you would like it. The mould then forms the basis from which the actual seat is made.

Invariably, seats are modified ad infinitum. This year, I used a remould of the seat I had in 1993 and, even then, I was continuing to make small alterations to it as the season went on. The seat itself is made from carbon fibre and covered with suede to prevent you from sliding around. It's thin but very strong and, if correctly made, gives perfect support and prevents bruising by spreading the load across your back.

The problem is that everything can feel fine for five laps or so. But, when you've been racing for an hour and a half, all sorts of things which did not concern you before can become very painful. You might find that the stitching on the inside of your overalls is rubbing you raw, or you may have your underpants in just the wrong place on your hips and that's creating discomfort. If anything like that occurs to you when driving, it means there must be a serious amount of pain because most difficulties are blanked out by the need to concentrate so hard.

Obviously, the last thing you want is to have your concentration disrupted at any stage during a race. An irritation could be caused by something such as the adjustment of the crotch straps, which come up between your legs. It is necessary to have them

tight enough to stop you from sliding around in the cockpit but, if they are too tight, then they will cut off the circulation to the legs after about twenty laps. And, if you can't feel your legs, you're out of the race.

You must focus your attention on all these things during the seat fitting; that is the time to discover any shortcomings and ask for changes to be made. Money is not a problem. You simply say, 'I want it done. I know it's going to be a drag to do this but I want it done that way because it's going to be important. It could possibly save us a race – and/or the championship.'

When I was with Brabham, the team was in terminal decline and it was not possible to have things done the way everyone would have liked. During the 1992 Hungarian Grand Prix, for example, there was a handling problem with the car and it oversteered. When I tried to correct one particularly bad slide by applying opposite lock, I couldn't get my hand past my leg, which meant I couldn't get enough lock on the steering and I spun off. There simply wasn't enough room in the cockpit. A driver must make sure that such a basic problem does not catch him out during the race.

Of course, it is not possible to appreciate fully some of these potential difficulties until the car is actually on the move. As I mentioned before, it often feels okay when sitting in the factory but it can be quite a different matter when you get to the circuit.

LOOK AND LEARN. I WATCH THE
MASTER — AYRTON SENNA

You begin to realize that your knuckles and elbows are banging against the sides of the cockpit as you try to operate at speed in such a restricted space.

The first outing in a new car tends to be a tedious affair. The mechanics and engineers are trimming and adjusting and, generally, the car doesn't feel right because you are not accustomed to it. Because the car is new, the first laps are about five seconds off the pace. This is a deliberate safety precaution. At the back of your mind is the thought that, from a design point of view, the car should be fine. Everything has been tested thoroughly at the factory; parts have been subjected to the rigours anticipated on the race track. And yet no one really knows if everything will be satisfactory when the car actually runs in anger. The first ten or fifteen laps tend to be a nailbiting occasion because something totally unexpected could occur which, for reasons no one can account for, might cause a failure.

As you do more and more laps, potential problems become obvious. The team is very, very thorough when they check the car. They notice tiny cracks and little things that need to be set right. You are concerned that there should be no abnormalities; you are watching for anything inexplicable.

From the outset, you are hoping to find that the new car is going to be better than the previous one. Maybe it will feel quicker out of the corners, perhaps it might have more downforce or possibly be faster on the straight because of a more slippery profile. You are talking about a minute percentage increase and yet, strange as it may seem, you can actually feel if the new car is better or not simply from your experience with the previous one.

When you are travelling at high speed you want the car to be as predictable as possible

After the preliminaries, you get down to serious business and begin to extract more performance from the car by fine-tuning the set-up. At first, you make fairly big changes, just to see what the effect is. It is an experiment, really, as you work with different springs, damper settings and important matters such as the ride height.

The distance between the bottom of the car and the ground is critical because this is where downforce is created. Adrian Newey and his team of aerodynamicists work hard at producing a car which generates as much downforce as possible, but without being sensitive to ride-height changes which could make the car undriveable.

The difficulty lies in the fact that the car is never riding at a constant height above the circuit because of the bumps in the track surface. And the other complication is that, the faster the car goes, the greater the effect of the downforce which squashes the car closer to the track – and thus changes the ride height even more. It is vital to have a car which does not get into a critical area at that low ride height level. We are talking about when you are travelling at high speed, when you want the car to be as predictable as possible. Changes of as little as one millimetre make a big difference to the behaviour of the car.

These are the sort of questions which a driver can't wait to have answered as he sits in the car for the first time in the factory, and this year was no exception. At the beginning of February Ayrton's FW16 was finished and shipped immediately to the Paul Ricard circuit in the south of France. I had to wait for a further couple of days while the mechanics worked flat out to complete my car. And when I finally got in it, I found I couldn't brake properly because there was not much room for my feet. I didn't manage very many laps and, all in all, that first test was hardly a success. My prime concern was to make it possible for me actually to drive the car.

I went straight back to the factory. With Adrian Newey and my engineer, John Russell, we set about discovering precisely why there was less room in FW16 than there had been in FW15. It is difficult to find a way of creating more space in such a confined area. My job is to make sure I can drive the car properly; it is up to the designers and engineers to find a solution. Adrian and John decided that certain modifications would improve the clearance for my feet and I felt a bit happier as we set off for Imola in Italy and the next phase of the test programme.

Initially, that turned out to be just as disappointing as Paul Ricard. I spent most of the first day standing around thanks to a number of technical problems which made it difficult to complete a consistent run. It was annoying because this was the first chance I would have to compare myself with Ayrton in the same car and under similar circumstances on the same track. Yet whenever the perfect situation presented itself, something would prevent us from running at the same time.

He would go out in the morning and not run in the afternoon; I would be immobile early in the day and out on the track when Ayrton was at a standstill. We were never out together. Nonetheless, I was only a tenth of a second slower than Ayrton on the first day. Then I would have to stand there and watch him take a

The times were displayed on a screen straddling the track and, when a Ferrari failed to do well, there would be a torrent of cheerful abuse

second and a half off my time because I had only managed a few laps. I would be itching to get out and establish exactly what I could do; see just how close I could get to his time.

It was very, very frustrating and I was extremely anxious not to let Ayrton stretch a gap on me. That sort of thing can be psychologically damaging; you only have to start thinking too much about a big time gap to your team-mate and, next thing, you begin to worry that it might not be bridgeable.

Of course, there was additional pressure being created by the fact that most of the top teams were also present at Imola. This may have been a test and not the Grand Prix (which would come at the end of April) but everyone was going very quickly; the times were close. The atmosphere was incredible because about 10,000 people turned up every day. The weather was beautiful, the grandstands were packed and, each time we went quickly, the fans would applaud – which was amazing considering this was Ferrari country. Of course, when a Ferrari appeared, there would be huge cheers from the grandstand opposite. The times were displayed on a screen straddling the track and, when a Ferrari failed to do well, there would be a torrent of cheerful abuse. It was a brilliant atmosphere thanks to such infectious enthusiasm; it really got you in the mood for the season.

By the end of the week, I had completed 140 laps and my time compared favourably with Ayrton's with the same amount of fuel on board and at the same time of day. The results which were released officially related to laps recorded at different times of the day, and of course took no account of the level of fuel being carried. This information is known only to the teams themselves and is kept a closely guarded secret in order to mislead (as much as possible) the opposition. What counted was the fact that I knew I was just a tenth of a second slower when it really mattered.

I came away reasonably encouraged. I felt good about my driving and good about the car – even if the pace of the Ferrari and the Benetton was cause for concern. I had managed to do some serious running with the car, blow away the winter cobwebs and familiarize myself with FW16.

All that was left was a short test run with one of the cars before shipment to Brazil. This took place in March on the short South Circuit at Silverstone and it was a lesson in why few teams try to conduct exhaustive tests in England during the winter. There were 50 mph gusts, coupled with hailstorms and showers. It was freezing cold; a far cry from what we could expect at most of the sixteen races to come.

We successfully practised refuelling stops for the first time and I was very impressed by the way the team had improved their pit stop technique. It is fair to say that Williams had been struggling from time to time when it came to conducting a quick tyre change in previous seasons, but it was apparent that they had been working hard on that during the winter.

Testing at somewhere like Silverstone in March can create a kind of vacuum which seals you from the world outside. There is no one there to bother you and it is easy to put your head down and get on with the job. You become totally immersed in the business of developing and testing; you quickly forget that thousands of people will be rooting for you to do well for Britain when you go to Brazil in two weeks' time.

I was unexpectedly brought back to reality when a press conference was called at the end of the test. It was a bit of a shock to step from the car and suddenly face a good turn-out of press people, anxious to put together their season previews. Having everyone come at once is satisfactory all round because it saves me saying the same thing over and over again and the press know they are guaranteed a story.

Nonetheless, a big gathering of journalists is a reminder of the interest in what you are doing and I must admit to suddenly getting a few butterflies.

It was a very good opportunity to talk about how I was approaching the season. I explained that this would be Ayrton Senna's eleventh year in Formula One and I hadn't even started racing when he won a Formula Three championship back in 1983. It was a chance to remind everyone that I would be racing with someone who was arguably one of the greatest drivers of all time.

But I also wanted to make it clear that I thought it was possible to beat him. I used the expression 'Sennaphobia' as a means of describing Ayrton's reputation for striking fear into a lot of drivers. I said that, in my opinion, that was a lot of hype; I didn't regard him as anything other than another racing driver – albeit a very good one.

This was not contrived bravado on my part. It was merely a reflection of the genuine feeling of optimism I had as the closed-season tests came to an end. I had gone through the winter without either damaging a car or having an incident through driver error. I was feeling bullish about the first race in Brazil. The only problem I had was a throat and chest infection which standing around in the freezing cold at Silverstone had done little to alleviate. But, otherwise, I had never been fitter. I was raring to go.

That changed as soon as I got to Brazil. The

This would be Senna's eleventh year in Formula One and I hadn't even started racing when he won a Formula Three championship back in 1983

CALM AMONG THE CLUTTER.
AN UNINHABITED CORNER OF
THE GARAGE PROVIDES A
WELCOME REFUGE FROM THE
PRE-QUALIFYING MADNESS. I USE
A SPECIAL WARM-UP TECHNIQUE
TO FOCUS THE MIND ON
WHAT LIES AHEAD

chest infection got worse and drained all of my energy. After so much training, I had arrived at the focal point of all those hours of running and weight-lifting – only to feel about as powerful as a damp handkerchief. It was with some misgiving that I set off on my first lap on the Friday morning.

Practice each day is split in two, with ninety minutes – separated by a fifteen-minute break at the half-way point – given over to so-called 'Free Practice' in the morning, followed by an hour of qualifying in the afternoon, when times count for the grid. The morning session is therefore dedicated to working on the car in preparation for qualifying and the race. Each driver is limited to just twenty-three laps, a tight restriction at the best of times but, in my case, something of a luxury on that Friday morning. I did not manage a single lap.

I had just left the pits when the fire extinguisher went off. That was an immediate let-down, made more difficult to accept by having to watch everyone else flying round, learning about their cars and the track. Then, once the cockpit had been cleaned up, to go out and have the car stop almost immediately with an electrical problem was tantamount to having someone completely pull the plug on you.

I felt the task had been difficult enough without all this. Now I had to go into the first qualifying session almost blind and establish a reasonable time in case it rained during the final qualifying session the following afternoon. Added to which, the car was

EXP :

ELF Solaize
FRANCE

very, very difficult to drive. All in all, the first day was fairly depressing.

After a lot of thought and planning during the subsequent debrief with my engineer, I felt optimistic about improving on my performance the following day. The aim was to get as close to Ayrton as I could during qualifying. I knew that I would be doing well to get on to the front row but third place, within a second of Ayrton's time, would be a very good performance, given the problems encountered the previous day.

Ultimately, to qualify fourth was, I thought, acceptable. At least I was in with a chance of doing well in the race. Ayrton and Michael Schumacher were on the front row and I knew I would have difficulty running with them.

I thought the only chance I had was to gamble by reducing the number of risks attached to making so many pit stops. With everyone adopting the same policy of making two refuelling stops, it seemed inevitable that the drivers would come in at the same time and that could cause a further delay. My car felt better with a heavier fuel load and I thought it would be an advantage to go out of phase with everyone else; I believed it would be possible to extract more of the car's potential over a longer period by making just one stop. From the outset, therefore, I was viewing this as a tactical race rather than one in which I could charge and attack.

But nothing prepared me for the pace at which Michael and Ayrton went off the line at the start. Added to which, Jean Alesi, third on the grid, made a good job of getting to the first corner

RIGHT NAME; RIGHT PLACE. AYRTON LEADS THROUGH THE APPROPRIATELY NAMED SENNA CURVES ON HIS HOME CIRCUIT

ahead of me. I could see from the fact that there were labels still on his tyres that the Ferrari had been fitted with a set of brand new slicks and it was obvious he was planning to really go for it by exploiting the advantage his new tyres would give him. Each car is given only seven sets (i.e., one set equals four tyres) of slick tyres for the whole race meeting, so for Alesi to have saved a set for the race meant he had sacrificed using a set for qualifying. It is entirely the driver's option as to how he intends to make best use of the tyres he is given. Goodyear supplies all the tyres for Formula One and at every meeting all the drivers use the same compound and construction, which is carefully selected by the Goodyear technicians based on years of experience of Formula One and track types.

Interlagos is abrasive and usually (as it was on this occasion) very hot due to the power of the Brazilian sun. A new set of tyres can be worth as much as one second per lap for four or five laps. Naturally, this is an advantage most teams would love to have. The downside is that new tyres can overheat and blister, effectively ruining a race. Nothing is for nothing, as they say! In this case, the advantage seemed to be worth having because I was now stuck behind Alesi. Not

It was then that I had to make a conscious decision about aiming to finish in the top three. The race was lost as far as I was concerned

only that, I was also struggling with the handling of the car. Meanwhile, Ayrton and the Benetton of Schumacher were disappearing rapidly.

It was then that I had to make a conscious decision about aiming to finish in the top three. The race was lost as far as I was concerned and my thoughts went back to earlier feelings about the first race of the season and the need to finish and get some points in the bag at this initial stage.

Part of the skill of being a racing driver is knowing your strong points and your weaknesses. I recognized on that particular day that I was a weak challenger rather than a strong one, so I aimed to come away with something rather than nothing at all. Indeed, that was a considerable test in itself because I was having quite a few problems with the car.

I would describe it as virtually undriveable in the slow corners and, in the quick ones, it threatened to turf you off the track at any moment. It was unpredictable, added to which there was a difficulty with a soft brake pedal. Without going into the technicalities, let me simply say that I ended up pressing the accelerator as well as the brake

– and that's not what you need at the end of the 190 mph straight, or anywhere else, for that matter.

I was having just about as many complications as you could wish to experience in a Grand Prix and the only consolation was that Alesi (whom I had passed by only having to stop once for fuel and twice for tyres) had dropped back and was not challenging me. As for Ayrton and Michael, they had lapped me before half distance. . .

Nonetheless, during pre-race calculations, I had considered the possibility of either Michael or Ayrton not finishing the race and, in truth, I suspected that the Benetton-Ford might let Schumacher down. In the event, the Williams got the better of Ayrton and he spun off five laps from the end.

Not long afterwards, I got into a slide at exactly the same corner. I managed to hold it but the team saw the moment on television and I was told to take it easy from then on. It was very much like the year before in Brazil. Alain Prost had spun off and I was the team's sole representative, holding second place, going for points for myself and helping the team in their quest for the constructors' championship. The only thing to do was concentrate on finishing and hope that the race would end as soon as possible.

I actually felt much better physically on the Sunday than I had during the previous two days. Josef, a physio who had joined the team with Ayrton, had been giving me the full treatment – acupuncture, massages, cough medicine, inhaling over a bucket of

'OY, MICHAEL, DRINK IT, DON'T
SPRAY IT!' TWO HAPPY BOYS
AFTER THE FIRST RACE

steaming eucalyptus with a towel over my head, anything and everything to try to pull me round – and I did feel the benefit of it on race day.

This was just as well because Interlagos is a punishing place. It gives you quite a shaking, and there is the additional problem of the track being dominated by left-hand corners, which means that the side of your neck which is favoured on the majority of race tracks elsewhere receives a lot of rough treatment.

I needed a massage afterwards. So did Ayrton. It was a measure of how difficult FW16 had been when he admitted that the car had exhausted him after an hour and a half of being battered and bruised while trying to keep everything under control. This was more a result of the car not being right than anything else. Whichever way you looked at it, Interlagos was very hard indeed.

It was not surprising that I should come away from Brazil with a smile on my face I knew that I had cashed in on a weekend when I really did not feel I was getting the best out of either the car or myself. And yet I was not particularly satisfied with the week-end overall.

Gary Player once said: 'The only people who remember you came second are your wife and your dog.' If that's the case, perhaps I should have thought about getting a dog! But the true significance of my second place (in a race in which my team-mate had not scored in his home Grand Prix!) is that I had avoided the nightmare repeat of the previous year, when I failed to finish the first race in South Africa. The championship was under way, Schumacher had won, but I was in contention. One down and fifteen to go.

CHAPTER FOUR
TRAVELLING THE WORLD
THE PACIFIC GRAND PRIX

Let's assume for a moment that the Grand Prix teams had never before raced in far-flung places such as Brazil and Japan. If you were to come along and suggest that fourteen teams could pack forty-two cars and 150 tons of equipment, fly to the other side of the world and, within a week, sort themselves out, hold a Grand Prix without a hitch, and then, twelve hours later, have everything ready to ship home again, you would be considered to be screaming mad. It just doesn't seem possible. And yet, each year we go to South America, Japan, Canada and Australia and, within a couple of days of each race, everything is back in Europe again, which is truly astounding when you consider the magnitude of the task.

Transport takes care of 10 per cent of the Williams team's budget. A large proportion of travel costs are accounted for by these so-called 'fly-away' races when the teams combine forces – under the aegis of the Formula One Constructors' Association (FOCA) – to charter a couple of jumbos to move every last nut and bolt. FOCA helps out the ten best-placed teams in the championship by providing a subsidy but, even so, there is no substitute for the amount of organization and hard work necessary to do the job.

If you ever get the chance to peer inside a Formula One garage, you will see it's full of small but important items

Ian Harrison, the team manager at Williams-Renault, has the task of making sure everything is in order. It is a heavy responsibility. There is no time for excuses if, halfway through a Grand Prix weekend, the team suddenly finds that some small but important item has been left at home. And if you ever get the chance to peer inside a Formula One garage, you will see it's full of small but important items.

The three things least likely to be forgotten are the race cars (one for each driver, plus a spare car) and, even then, these are a barely recognizable part of the cargo. The wide wheels we use to race on are removed and special wheels – rather like those you would find on a motor cycle – are put in their place. They look most strange but these wheels take up less room and yet still allow the cars to be moved about as they are loaded on to pallets, ready to go into the aeroplane.

The nose and rear wing will have been taken off, along with other easily removed

TRAVELLING THE WORLD

and breakable parts. There will be padding and protective pieces of plywood placed outside the side pods and the car will be covered with a specially made tarpaulin with aircraft straps on the top to allow the whole thing to be picked up.

Everything else goes into boxes, known as packhorses. Williams took sixty of them to Japan for the Pacific Grand Prix last April. Multiply that lot by fourteen – granted, some of the smaller teams will not carry as much equipment – and you begin to get some idea of the enormity of the task. Some of these boxes are huge. They must be large enough to take spare floors and, obviously, these are as big as the car itself. The floors look like massive sheets of plywood, except they are made of carbon fibre and they go into these volume boxes, so-called because they are so big that you pay for the size of the box rather than its weight.

It has not been unknown for a vital piece of equipment – such as an engine – to be left on the tarmac simply because the right form had not been filled in

When we went to the Pacific Grand Prix in Japan, Williams took nine spare floors and these were part of the team's fifteen-ton payload. We had everything in there: kits of tools, work surfaces, body parts, repair kits (resin for the carbon fibre), computers, calculators, colour screens, printers, generators, voltage regulators, compressors and a few hundred kilogrammes of miscellaneous items such as screws, fasteners, tape and scissors. We even took spares to repair the boxes themselves, the smaller bits and pieces being stored in plastic trays which are slotted into makeshift drawers.

For Japan we had to take at least twenty sets of wheels. The tyres themselves are shipped by Goodyear and, similarly, Renault takes care of our engines, each one in a special box on wheels to allow for easy movement around the back of the garage. Our fuel is supplied by Elf and, since that has to be blended in France, not only for each type of engine, but also for each type of circuit, the end-product has to be specially shipped out for the race. I can't imagine what it must be like to fly a plane carrying countless gallons of volatile fuel; I can only suppose that these pilots think people who drive racing cars are just as crazy.

Of course, the introduction of refuelling in 1994 meant we also had to add further bulky equipment to our freight. The refuelling rig is a gigantic affair which looks like a kidney dialysis machine or some strange sort of diving equipment. The container is five foot tall by three foot square with pipes and hoses coming out of it in all directions. And each team has to take at least two of these around the world.

All of this means a huge amount of extra work. It takes something like three and a half days – flat out – to pack. Everything must be weighed carefully and recorded, otherwise the team leaves itself open for an additional bill for excess baggage – and we're not talking about the extra few kilos which come with a stuffed suitcase. The customs paperwork will have been sorted out – again, with great care. It has not been unknown for a vital piece of equipment – such as an engine – to be left on the tarmac simply because the right form had not been filled in.

Ian Harrison and Dickie Stanford, our chief mechanic, will fly out a day early with four mechanics – usually the truck crews – in order to begin setting up. The boxes will have been deposited in no particular order around the garage and it is up to the boys to get busy with a fork-lift truck and arrange this sprawling collection of blue packhorses into some sort of order. They will check for damage and generally make sure everything has arrived before beginning to unpack.

One of the first jobs, however, is to paint the garage floor – a fairly recent

THE BIG 'O'. ROY ORBISON IS
SPOTTED, ALIVE AND WELL AND
LIVING AS A JAPANESE MARSHAL
IN AIDA

LONG DISTANCE DEDICATION.
AIDA MAY BE SOME WAY FROM
THE CITIES BUT A GRAND PRIX IS
STILL A GRAND PRIX AND THE
JAPANESE FANS ARE AS KEEN
AS MUSTARD

innovation in the bid to make the garages look spick and span – and then erect the background awnings which carry the sponsors' names. All this should be made ready by the time the rest of the team arrives that evening. In theory, the mechanics should then be able to launch straight into building and preparing the cars for the start of practice a few days later.

By the time I arrive, on the day before practice begins, the place really looks like home from home. Of course, on the fly-away races the team does not have the comfort and the convenience of the trucks and motorhomes which attend the races in Europe. We have to make do with temporary offices at the back of the garage. There will be space for us somewhere but it tends to be a little bit more ramshackle on fly-away races.

The worst one seems to be Suzuka in Japan where everyone has to work from construction-site-type offices which are held together by scaffolding poles and stacked one on top of the other. Everyone tries their best to operate in these situations but it is quite

difficult; it just adds to the pressure as you cope with the additional problem of jet-lag and being so far from base.

ORIENTAL BLOOM: CHERRY

BLOSSOM IS BIG IN JAPAN

Compared to this, the races in Europe are usually very slick from an operational point of view. All you need is the garage and thereafter everything else is contained within the trucks (two for Williams and two for Renault) you take to the races. Our so-called race truck has a debrief room which is big enough to take all the engineers and the drivers. It's sound-proof which means we can sit down in reasonable comfort and have discussions without being disturbed. The rest of the space in that truck is given over to gearbox work at the races.

All three cars are brought to the track in the second truck and, once they are removed, the mechanics and the engineers have a fully-fitted workshop at their disposal. Most of the tools are stored in cabinets which are bolted to the truck floor, but these units can then be removed at the circuit and wheeled into place in the garage. All of this adds to the impression of cleanliness and orderliness which is very much the standard expected of Grand Prix teams these days.

It wasn't always so, of course. Twenty years ago, everything would literally be thrown into one truck and the team would muddle through at the other end. Garages were unheard of and the teams had to work under an awning hung from the side of the transporter. With all the equipment necessary now, the teams couldn't cope with that sort of arrangement, particularly the engine manufacturers with their vast array of telemetry.

Renault brings two trucks, one with a debrief room and the screens and computers ready to receive information from the cars, and the other containing the engines themselves. Added to all this is a third small truck from Williams which carries bodywork and the floors I described earlier which, although not particularly heavy, are bulky and awkward because of being made in one piece.

Cleanliness and orderliness is very much the standard expected of Grand Prix teams these days

Finally there are the motorhomes, one each for Williams, Renault and the principal sponsor, Rothmans. So, all in all, it's quite a train. And we're talking about just one team. This is the way you need to operate because it means you can more or less prepare a little factory away from home.

The trucks can take anything up to three days to reach the far-flung events such as Hungary and Portugal but, once there, they simply plug into the mains electricity, the water and the telephone lines. The rest of us can fly out in a day and as soon as we walk into the garage there is a feeling that it is a permanent fixture. Everything will be in place; the familiar logos will be on the walls and all of the fifty-strong travelling team will be toiling away.

It may seem like a recipe for chaos but everything has its place. Apart from the floor space designated for working on the three cars, there will be areas set aside to allow the watching of video screens, computer screens and so on. Frank Williams likes to have his own bank of screens showing television pictures of the cars in action as well as lap times and speed trap figures. Meanwhile, out at the pit wall, a tubular platform will have been erected to accommodate the engineers as they watch another bank of monitors as well as the action on the track.

Compared to all this, the driver's preparation at the race track is relatively simple. Apart from discussions with his engineer about the technical programme they intend to work through, all the driver has to do is get dressed for action. In Europe that is easy thanks to a changing room in one of the trucks. Further afield, it is a matter of changing in the garage or the Portakabin, which can be pretty basic. But most drivers don't mind because that's the way it was when they started racing in the junior formulae. In my case, I used to get changed in the back of a transit van and, in a way, you were happy to do that. It was not a problem. It is the same with the fly-away races because you accept there are not many trimmings and you just get on with it.

The nice thing about racing in Europe is that you are just that little bit more familiar with the place. You can arrive on the Thursday, not get to the circuit until lunchtime and yet that will be time enough. But, on the fly-away races, invariably you need to go out early in order to get over your jet-lag. You try to relax, but you can't.

I find it very difficult to sleep on planes. I've thought about sleeping pills but the problem is you daren't take anything like that because it could be in your system for weeks and you don't want to make yourself drowsy. Perhaps that's okay on the way home but, even then, I'm wary of taking sleeping pills because I might be testing a few days after my return. The best plan is just to let plain exhaustion knock me out.

Apart from discussions with his engineer, all the driver has to do is get dressed for action

On the way to the races, I'd rather travel during the day and arrive without losing any sleep but getting comfortable on aircraft is simply impossible. Because of my height, I end up sticking pillows under my back, behind my head; everywhere really. But it makes no difference. I travel Business Class usually. It's horribly expensive – if you're lucky, you can get an upgrade – but you need to do as much as possible to help yourself arrive in good shape. Flying really can take it out of you.

It can be particularly bad coming home from a Grand Prix, especially if you have not had a chance to take a shower immediately after the race. Your neck will be pretty stiff and when you get on the plane, there is air conditioning blowing down on you. You have got to be very careful not to get muscle cramp or a problem with your neck at times like that.

Generally, though, you are either excited about going to a race or you are keen to get home. Either way, I'm not too worried about flying; I quite enjoy it. Usually the entire plane is booked out to Formula One personnel and getting any sleep – particularly on the way to a race – is out of the question because everyone is standing around and chatting.

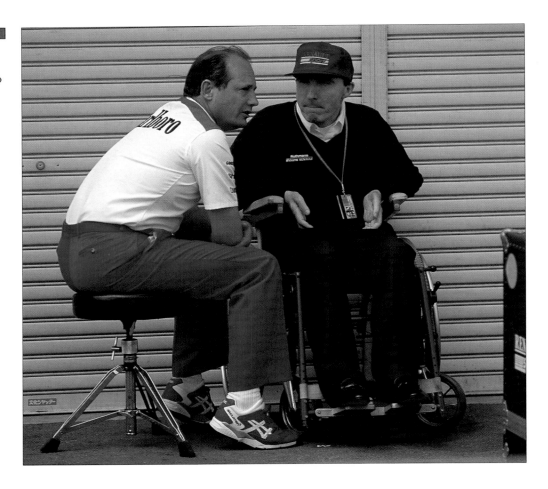

POWER BROKING.

RON DENNIS FROM MCLAREN AND

MY BOSS FRANK WILLIAMS PLAN

THE NEXT MOVE

That's certainly the case en route to the first race of the season in Brazil. Everyone will want to talk and exchange information and it is an opportunity to get to see people you wouldn't normally have the chance to talk to at length. It's a good, friendly atmosphere, similar to being on a coach filled with people you know.

Having said all that, Jon Nicholson and I didn't see many people we knew when we flew out early for the Pacific Grand Prix. After the problems of Brazil, I wanted everything to be absolutely right for this race and the purpose of the advance arrival was to allow plenty of time to acclimatize. We explored the north coast of Japan and ended up in a sand dune in the middle of a Force 10 gale, a massive contrast to the serenity of a Buddhist temple which we visited a few days later half-way up a mountain somewhere.

I seem to get recognized everywhere I go in Japan now. The fans always have a camera and they like to take pictures, not just of you but they will get someone to take a picture of them and you. And they have whopping big autograph tiles which are

THE PACIFIC GRAND PRIX

similar to those insulation plates on which you put your kettle in the kitchen. I really don't know why they have them because, if you've got ten of them, you've got quite a big stack and that, I would have thought, is not what you need in homes which tend to be very small. I just don't know where they put them.

The Japanese are mad about Grand Prix racing. As Jon and I flew from Tokyo to Okayama, there were two girls sitting behind us. One of them said, 'You're Damon Hill, you're with Williams.' Then she said, 'I'm so excited, I'm going to throw up!' That was the extent of her English. We asked her to hang on if she could, because we hadn't even taken off! That's how excited they get.

Our hotel for race weekend very rarely had Westerners as guests and they were completely freaked out at having Formula One people come to stay, particularly Ayrton Senna. It got to the point where they closed down the restaurant because they were terrified that they might not be able to serve what we liked. So, they took the easy way out and, rather than embarrass themselves, they told us to have supper in another

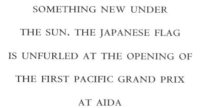

SOMETHING NEW UNDER
THE SUN. THE JAPANESE FLAG
IS UNFURLED AT THE OPENING OF
THE FIRST PACIFIC GRAND PRIX
AT AIDA

BERGER DRIVING A BEAUTIFUL

BIG RED CAR

hotel. The next race at Imola would appear to be like home turf by comparison.

Because the TI circuit at Aida was new in every sense, we were allowed an additional day of practice in order to find our way around. Learning an unfamiliar track is not as difficult as you might imagine because, after a few years spent going round the circuits of the world, you recognize corners which have similar characteristics and you tackle them more or less the same way.

The main job on a new track is becoming familiar with the potential hazards which might catch you out on a particular corner; things such as kerbs that it might be advisable to avoid; bumps in the surface which could cause the car to bottom momentarily and give you a fraction of a second of understeer or oversteer.

Checking out the circuit on foot beforehand is important. It is simply not possible, when you go round in a Formula One car at speed, to detect what it is that causes the bumps. When you walk round you can see quite clearly that there may be a part of the track with a different surface and you can actually feel the bump. Or perhaps you can examine it just as you would when sizing up a snooker shot; you can get down to track level and have a good look and come away with the opinion that it's worth taking extra care at that particular corner. Also, you get to recognize what sort of track surface it is, how much dust there is off line and things like that.

Sometimes, it must be said, you are better off not knowing too much about the

DO WHAT? RON DENNIS LISTENS
TO MIKA HAKKINEN'S COMMENTS
AND TRIES TO INTERPRET THEM
INTO ENGINEER LANGUAGE

circuit. At Aida, for example, the second corner did not have an adequate gravel run-off area. If you left the road at that point then you would hit the wall at almost 90 degrees. While lapping in a Formula One car, you wouldn't notice that. But if you knew about the potential problem and it caused you concern, then you are well advised to forget about it because you would not perform well if you were worried about crashing on a particular corner.

At Aida the second corner did not have an adequate gravel run–off area. If you left the road at that point then you would hit the wall at almost 90 degrees

When you are in an Formula One car, it is almost as if you drive internally. You need to see where you're going, of course, but you concentrate on the sensations you are receiving from the car. I reckon it took most people only about twenty or thirty laps to learn the circuit because, to be honest, Aida was not super-quick and a lot of the corners were fairly similar.

There were only ten corners; not enough to confuse you. Certainly not like circuits such as the Isle of Man T.T. course or the old Nurburgring in Germany, places where it was a job to know whether the road went straight on or turned sharp right or left over the next blind brow.

Even Suzuka, scene of the Japanese Grand Prix later in the year, was difficult enough when I went there for the first time. There is a series of left-right-left-right curves

and I found that I couldn't remember exactly which left- or right-hand curve I was in; you can waste five or six laps simply familiarizing yourself. Suzuka also has the additional difficulty of being one of the longest tracks we race on. The number of laps is consequently reduced and the actual lap time is longer. As a result, the greater the length of time spent between seeing the corner each time, the more difficult it is to get it right.

You can try different lines and look out for places where you can steal a bit of track to help your speed through the corner. But, again, you may not realize you can use that piece of road unless you have walked round the track. There might be a white line painted on what appears to be the edge and yet there's plenty of tarmac between the white line and the grass. You may not be able to pick up on that when you're going through at 120 mph. The problem is you need to look quite a long way ahead – maybe 200 yards or so – and that means you can't determine the exact nature of the part of the track you are actually on.

It is also useful watching the other cars go round. The TV coverage gives some clues because you can see what happens if someone uses one part of the track rather than another. But, all told, there were few problems at Aida. The main object was to find the quickest way round and I was pretty pleased that I had qualified less than half a second behind Ayrton Senna on pole position, because it was as good a place as any of Ayrton's team-mates had managed in the past.

I had been confident that the difference between myself and Ayrton was less than it had appeared in Brazil and I wanted the opportunity for that to come out in public. Practice for the Pacific Grand Prix had backed up my belief.

There was also the thought that Senna had failed to score in Brazil whereas I was only four points behind Michael Schumacher. Even if Ayrton was to win in Japan and I finished second again, I would still be ahead of him in the championship. More than anything, I wanted to capitalize on that six-point head-start I had earned in Brazil.

But, having said that, I was in two minds about how to run the Pacific Grand Prix. My original strategy – to score as many points as possible in the opening races of the season – still stood. On the other hand, this seemed like a good opportunity to push the boat out and compensate for Brazil, a race I wasn't happy about, despite the final result.

The main object was to find the quickest way round and I was pretty pleased that I had qualified less than half a second behind Ayrton

Either way, I was confident on race morning. My car had felt fantastic during the warm-up and, whereas it had been easy for me to achieve my lap time, I could see that it had been more difficult for Ayrton to establish a time which was less than a tenth of a second quicker than me. The thought of leading a Grand Prix again was very attractive even though I was starting from the second row, behind Senna and Schumacher.

It all went wrong straightaway. I made a dreadful start. It was one of those infuriating occasions when I thought the lights were changing – but they weren't. And, of course, the instant you stop rolling forward and come off the throttle – on comes the green light. I dropped the clutch far too quickly, got loads of wheelspin and was completely helpless as cars came whistling past. But, just as I was thinking I had made a right mess of everything, things went my way again.

Going into the first corner, there was a bit of confusion ahead of me as Mika Hakkinen tapped the back of Ayrton's car and sent the Williams into a spin. For one

AYRTON BURNS RUBBER. MICHAEL
SCHUMACHER PULLS CLEAR

terrible moment I thought I might actually hit him. But, mercifully, the Williams team was spared an instant wipe-out as I managed to scrape through. And, not only that, as others in front of me ducked and dived, I stayed on course and regained the places I had lost at the start! I was third, behind Schumacher and Hakkinen. Ayrton was out of the race.

Even so, there was some rapid reassessing going on as I weighed up the latest position. Before the start, we had guessed (correctly, as it turned out) that Michael would be stopping twice for fuel and tyres. We worked out that stopping three times

would be the best way forward for Williams-Renault – but only if we were ahead of the traffic and able to fly on a clear track during the opening laps. I usually make good starts and I felt confident I could stay with Ayrton – who was also planning to stop three times – and, together, we would pull away from Michael. But here I was, third, with Schumacher disappearing into the distance. The plan was falling apart and I needed to get past Hakkinen at the earliest opportunity.

The plan was falling apart and I needed to get past Hakkinen at the earliest opportunity

The hairpin at the end of the straight seemed, on paper, an unlikely overtaking place. But I had worked out that, because the corner was banked, it might be possible to go round the outside of the McLaren through the right-hander and then be on the inside for the left-hander which followed. He would have to back off because I would be on the right line. That was the theory.

Unfortunately, he didn't back off. Rather than hit him I decided to go across the kerb. The car half-spun and stopped. I kept the engine going and managed to get away but, by now, my tyres had picked up all sorts of rubbish and that cost me a few more places as the car slithered all over the place until the tyres were clean again.

The first thing that comes into your mind is that this is going horribly wrong. And then you think, 'Well, the least I can do is give it everything and come away from the race with a drive I would be proud of.' Besides, I was running with a comparatively light load of fuel and was therefore ideally placed to overtake.

There is nothing more invigorating than passing people. Even if you don't win, the race can be memorable simply because you have been moving forward while everyone else seems to be going backwards. I pulled some good moves and really got into

a rhythm as I worked my way into second place. Of course, there was always the thought that I was going to have to stop early for more fuel and then face the task of doing it all again. But, even so, the charge through the field on the second occasion was just as rewarding.

Not so satisfying was the fact that I was making no impression on Schumacher. I was only just holding the gap steady. It quickly became apparent that we were beaten – for the second race in succession. That can be quite demoralizing, to say the least. You try to work out where he is quicker and then you do everything you can but, if you

A GOOD DRIVE CUT SHORT

can't go any faster, then you have to face the fact that you'll never catch him. Even so, my original plan – to score as many points as possible at the beginning of the season – was still in place. Six points for another second place would do nicely.

I was having one or two problems with the car at that stage (too much understeer, which meant the car wanted to go straight on at the corners, and a sticking throttle which meant the power would come in a rush a split second later than anticipated) but the last thing I expected was to have the car actually break down. Suddenly, after forty-five of the eighty-three laps, there was no drive to the rear wheels and I coasted to a halt.

After all that effort; after coming out early, carefully preparing myself and showing well during practice; after passing more cars than anyone else in the race and working my way into second place – twice; after all of that I was going home with a big zero. And Schumacher had won again. It was a disappointing end to an interesting, if rather lengthy, week in Japan.

But the local people could not have been nicer. At the end of the first day of practice, I had been quickest and they all lined up on my return to offer congratulations and

AS AYRTON WATCHES THE RACE
WE BOTH SHOULD HAVE BEEN IN,
ALL I CAN THINK IS 'LET'S GET
THESE WET THINGS OFF AND GET
THE HELL BACK HOME!'

SOMETIMES IT'S A STRUGGLE TO
FIND ADEQUATE WORDS . . .

bow. When we finally left the hotel, one of the women came out and waved and bowed. As we crossed the nearby river, I looked back from the far end of the bridge – and she was still waving, We had been gone about three or four minutes and yet I could still see her in the distance, waving enthusiastically. The way they received us had been very touching and that was a nice send-off for the long trek home.

Someone has worked out that a Formula One team can clock up 100,000 miles every year, during which time we each spend roughly 200 hours in an aeroplane. After the journey to the Pacific Grand Prix and back, I felt I had done half of the annual mileage during a single trip.

CHAPTER FIVE

THE BLACKEST WEEKEND

THE SAN MARINO GRAND PRIX

A POIGNANT CONTRAST TO WHAT

WAS TO COME AT IMOLA

The first shock came when Rubens Barrichello crashed during the opening qualifying session at Imola. He lost control of his Jordan coming through the last chicane, probably at around 140 mph, and didn't have time to correct the car. He shot over a kerb, which launched him into the air and then sent the Jordan barrel-rolling along the tyre barrier.

What shook us most was the rate at which the car took off; at one stage it looked as if it was going to smash through the fence and fly into the grandstand. The Jordan, more by luck than anything else, finished on its side, upside down and against the barrier. That was bad enough but the marshals promptly tipped the car over and, as it crashed on to its bottom, you could see Barrichello's head thrashing around in the cockpit.

I was astonished that the marshals should have done that, particularly in view of the neck and spinal injuries received by J. J. Lehto and Jean Alesi during test sessions earlier in the year. After an accident like that, Barrichello could have sustained similar injuries. He should have been left as he was or, if there was a risk of fire, then at least the car should have been put down gently.

The next day, Rubens was walking around the paddock with nothing more than a cut lip and a broken nose. He was talking about making a come-back at the next race. The incident, despite its worrying implications, was gradually forgotten as Grand Prix racing got back down to business. In our case, that meant continuing our efforts to improve the Williams FW16.

Despite having tested at Nogaro in the south-west of France during the days leading up to Imola, we were still concerned about FW16. There had been a certain amount of educated guesswork and, while everyone tried to be optimistic, Ayrton and I were sceptical; we couldn't honestly say that the car was going to be any better than it had been.

The problem was, in essence, two-fold. First, the car was not consistently quicker than the Benetton and, second, it felt horrible to drive. It is arguable as to which of the two problems made Ayrton and myself more unhappy, but it was most probably the former.

Ayrton had enormous reserves of ability and could overcome deficiencies in a chassis

We were always changing the set-up of the car in an attempt to find that perfect combination which would turn the promise of a great car into a reality. What we wanted from the FW16 was a feeling of balance and driveability. These are the conditions which enable a driver to enjoy the experience of driving and, consequently, go faster. It is difficult to become familiar with a car if it is constantly being changed in an attempt to get good performance – it becomes a vicious circle.

Ayrton, however, had enormous reserves of ability and could overcome deficiencies in a chassis. Also, it is more common to have a car which is difficult than one which is perfect. So, in some ways, things were as they should have been at Imola.

It was a pleasant surprise to find on the first day of practice that things had improved slightly. I was looking forward to really making some progress with the car even though I had one or two nerve-racking moments when I had to take to the grass because of a difficulty with the brakes. Patrick Head pointed out that, if there was a way of doing things wrong, then I appeared to be doing it! I was suitably chastened by his dressing down although I felt better at the end of the day when it was discovered that there had indeed been a problem with my car.

With Barrichello we had been lucky. This time it was very clear that poor Roland was not going to be let off so lightly

I had gone off at the final corner and damaged the suspension. By the time repairs had been carried out, there were just ten minutes of the first qualifying session remaining and I only managed seventh place on the provisional grid. Even so, I still felt good about the Williams although I can't honestly say that Ayrton shared my optimism; he was not convinced we were going in the right direction. In other words, he didn't like certain aspects of the car's behaviour. But then he was a perfectionist.

A lot of thought was put into the set-up and, on Saturday, the car really was much better. On my first quick laps during qualifying, I managed to pull myself up to fourth place. It had been a decent run and I was on my way in when I came across warning flags at the end of the 200 mph straight. I got to Tosa corner, only to be confronted by the remains of Roland Ratzenberger's Simtek.

I could see where the debris had started and, judging by the distance travelled, it was obvious that this had been a very big accident. As I went by, I had a strong sense of foreboding about his condition because there was so much destruction. With Barrichello we had been lucky. This time it was very clear that poor Roland was not going to be let off so lightly. And, unbeknown to everyone, this was to be the start of a terrible sequence of events which would demonstrate in no uncertain terms the inherent dangers of the sport.

Practice was stopped. Ayrton went down to the site of the accident because he wanted to see for himself what had happened. He had done it before when Martin Donnelly crashed at Jerez in 1990 and I believe it is every driver's right to do that sort of thing if they wish. Personally, I would rather not. I had been present at Goodwood during a Formula Three test session in February 1986 when Bertrand Fabi was killed and I had no wish to see anything like that again.

Anyway, Ayrton chose to go to Tosa. Everyone was terribly concerned for Roland; the feeling was that he was in a bad way. When Ayrton returned, he spoke to Patrick and me in private at the side of the motorhome. He said quite simply that Roland was dead. It was his way of getting the point across to us as deliberately as possible that from what he had witnessed there was no doubt about it. Then he went into the motorhome and changed out of his driving overalls even though the session was about to re-start.

I could not decide what the right thing to do should be; stop like Ayrton or soldier on? I wished the officials had cancelled the rest of the session so as to remove that particular dilemma. It had been left to me to decide whether or not I wished to go out again. You are immediately confronted with the question, 'Do I get back into a racing car now – tomorrow – a week later – or never again?' Just how do you decide?

It's not as if racing drivers don't know that fatal accidents are a possibility. If a driver does not accept that fact, if he is completely and utterly shocked by an accident like Ratzenberger's, so much so that he cannot get back in a racing car, then he has been deluding himself about the danger up until that point.

Of course, racing drivers are not that stupid. But, when confronted with something like this, you are facing a severe and immediate test of whether or not you are prepared to accept the risk. Roland had said he was never as happy as when he got his Formula One drive. It's what he wanted to do. It's what a lot of people want to do and many never get the opportunity. Even so, that does not make situations such as this any easier to accept.

Everyone was deeply affected by Roland's death. Williams and Benetton withdrew for the rest of the afternoon; others decided to continue with the session. But the question everyone was asking was, 'Why did Roland die?' There was concern that we had got to the point where the inherent risks in Formula One had become greater

ROLAND RATZENBERGER
GAVE UP EVERYTHING TO BECOME
A FORMULA ONE DRIVER.
HE DESERVED MORE OF A CHANCE

because of certain factors such as the speed of the cars and their increasing ability to withstand impacts. Something has to give and, in the light of recent accidents, it was turning out to be the driver.

Had we reached the totally unacceptable stage where, if a car was going to hit a wall then the driver was going to die? Ironically, in the light of what would happen the following day, Ayrton went to talk with other drivers and people such as Niki Lauda, who had been involved in a horrific accident in 1976. They wanted to know what could be done – and done immediately – about safety. It was agreed that the drivers should meet and discuss these matters, probably at Monaco in two weeks' time.

The mood that night was sombre to say the least. I stayed at the circuit, ate at the motorhome and generally found it difficult to think of much else but the accident. I tried to concentrate hard on what we were going to do for the race. My thoughts were, 'Look, I'm not going to stop racing; I'm looking forward to the Grand Prix. I enjoy my motor racing just as Roland did. Every second you are alive, you've got to be thankful and derive as much pleasure from it as you can.' In some ways, events that afternoon had been a spur, a reminder not to become complacent. It prompted me to be as positive as I could, look forward to the race and pray that something could be done to prevent such things happening again. It was to be a short-lived hope.

When the cars went out for the warm-up on race morning, it was the first time I had been on the circuit since knowing the outcome of Roland's accident. It was terrifying to go past the point where he had crashed. You could suddenly imagine the force of the impact because you were actually travelling at the same speed he had been doing before he went off.

Under normal circumstances, you wouldn't give it a second thought because, even though speeds reach 200 mph, it is not a part of the circuit where you come close to the limit; it is not a place you would worry about. You are relying entirely on the car and, in the light of Roland's accident (probably caused by a failure of the nose wing mounting), it brings it home that sometimes you are just a passenger, putting your faith in the components.

It feels very uncomfortable placing all your trust in the machinery — but there is no alternative

Drivers can accept the penalty of making a mistake; there is always the hope that they can do something about retrieving the situation and that the penalty is not too severe. At least it's their mistake. However, it feels very uncomfortable placing all your trust in the machinery – but there is no alternative. It is rather like being on an aeroplane; you are at the mercy of the pilot and the integrity of the equipment. You are powerless to do anything about your situation. At least I had the consolation of driving for Williams Grand Prix Engineering. I knew they would always do the best job possible.

I knew, too, that Ayrton was out to dominate proceedings on race day. He had been fastest during the warm-up and I was next, 9/10ths of a second slower. I was happy with the car and I knew exactly what I'd had to do to set that time. So it was clear that Ayrton must have tried very hard indeed to set his time.

It seemed to me that my team-mate was playing a psychological game here because, when you know that someone is almost a second a lap faster, it can demoralize you before the race has even started. I was not too worried because I was happy with the pace I was running at; I knew I could keep that up throughout the race whereas I didn't think Ayrton could. It was going to be a very interesting race.

All of this kept my mind focused on the job but, when we went to the pre-race

RENAULT POWER UNDER WRAPS

drivers' briefing, the previous day's tragedy proved to be just beneath the surface of everyone's consciousness. There was a minute's silence for Roland and the atmosphere was heavy with more than the usual pre-race tension. The talk of a drivers' meeting about safety to take place before Monaco rang alarm bells with the Formula One organizers. Whenever drivers group together there is the potential for trouble. Well, we were all together now, in the pre-race drivers' briefing as usual, and we weren't happy. But there was very little that could actually be achieved right then. Gerhard Berger raised one seemingly insignificant but relevant point about safety. But what he did not reveal was that he had been put up to it by Senna. Ayrton didn't want to be the first to raise the point for fear of appearing to be the only person concerned about the problem, yet, typically, it was he who pressed it home.

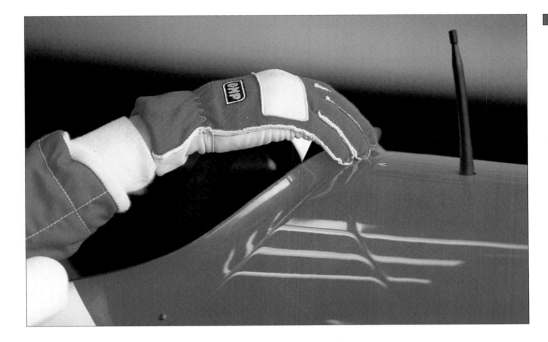

One of the things which had upset Ayrton in Japan had been the introduction of a pace car during the final parade lap leading to the start. He felt that it was nothing more than a gimmick and contributed nothing else than making the cars run far too slowly and therefore less able to put heat into their tyres. When other drivers backed him up, the officials agreed without hesitation to abandon that idea. A small victory had been won, but it was nonetheless significant.

The talk of a drivers' meeting about safety to take place before Monaco rang alarm bells with the Formula One organizers

This was evidence of a failure to consult the drivers on important issues. There are certain matters which only the drivers are qualified to comment on and this strengthened the view that we should get together and express our fears in an attempt to have things changed and make the racing a little bit safer.

As the race approached, I'm sure most drivers were able to put those thoughts to the back of their minds. I think everyone felt – as they had done for the previous twelve years – that the dangers had been reduced considerably, to the point where death was but a slim possibility. And, in the aftermath, it was felt that Roland's crash had been one accident in a decade and it was unlikely to happen again for a while. You could claim that it is stupid to act like that. But that's the way people think.

In any case, I'm sure Ayrton had other things to occupy him at this stage. Pressure

THE SAN MARINO GRAND PRIX

had been coming from all directions. The media had been making a point about how the winner at Imola nearly always goes on to take the championship; that Ayrton had failed to score a single point in the first two races (something he had never experienced before in his ten years in Formula One); that Michael Schumacher was the coming man and had a twenty-point lead over Ayrton; that this was a crucial race because Schumacher and Benetton were favourites to win the next round at Monaco. I think all of that had impressed itself upon Ayrton. The warm-up had shown he was in a fighting mood. He had pole position and he was raring to turn the tide.

Some people have attempted to infer that Ayrton was not in the right frame of mind for the race, but I cannot say anything more than that, to me, he seemed totally focused. It must have been difficult completely to ignore the events of the day before, even for a man such as Ayrton, but when a race is about to start your mind can be on one thing only – winning.

Sure enough, he made a good start but we only got as far as the Acque Minerali chicane at the top of the circuit when the red flags came out and there were signs that the safety car was being brought into play. The safety car had been a fairly recent innovation, a means of slowing the field as it formed behind an official car and circulated at reduced pace until whatever problem on the track had been sorted out. In this case, when we got to the start/finish area, we could see there had been a collision.

J. J. Lehto, starting from the second row, had stalled and had been hit from behind by Pedro Lamy who had performed some sort of extraordinary manoeuvre from the penultimate row and crashed into the back of the Benetton.

I had been warned on the radio that there was a lot of wreckage on the track but I was not aware that a wheel and parts of a car had cleared the fence and gone into the enclosure, injuring a number of spectators. There was debris everywhere and it was difficult to avoid it, which was a worry.

The aim of the safety car is to keep the show going without bringing the race to a complete halt. But my feeling was that this should only have applied during a race once it was up and running. In this case, we hadn't even done a full lap at racing speed and it was difficult to see why the race could not have been stopped and re-started, as permitted by the rules. The net result was that we were forced to go round at what can only be described as a snail's pace for five laps.

Anyone who has worked with Ayrton will tell you how much time and effort he

put in to making sure his tyre pressures were absolutely right. I'm not exaggerating when I say that he could tell, to within half a pound psi, whether the car was balanced or not. This is a critical area because every racing car is sensitive to tyre pressures. While we wait on the grid during the final fifteen minutes or so, the tyres are wrapped in electric warmers and these ensure that the temperatures are maintained, even during the minute or so after the blankets

My car was more difficult to drive than usual during those first few laps after the re-start

have been removed and we wait for the green flag. But the problem is that, during the subsequent parade lap, the pressures and temperatures drop due to the fact that you are not running quickly enough to generate sufficient heat in the rubber. And, as Ayrton had pointed out, this business of running the Porsche pace car in Japan only made matters worse.

During the first few laps of the race, therefore, the car does not handle particularly well until the heat gets back into the tyres and the pressures come up. And at Imola, the problem was compounded when we had to do five laps behind the safety car. Certainly, my car was more difficult to drive than usual during those first few laps after the re-start.

To be honest, I hadn't helped matters by messing up the re-start slightly when the safety car pulled off. It so happened that, on the two occasions when the safety car had been used in the past, I had been leading. The trick is to drop back and give yourself a free run once the car disappears but, when you are in traffic, as I was at Imola, it is not possible to see exactly where the safety car is. It is best to stick with the guys in front but, in this instance, I had dropped back too much and, when Ayrton and Michael took off at the re-start, I was already about five seconds behind.

But I had learned an important lesson. At Imola, there is a tight chicane just before the start/finish straight. When I slowed for the chicane, the brakes and the tyres

were cold. I locked up my left-front wheel and, for a terrible moment, I thought I was going to slide off the road before I had even started the first flying lap. That alerted me to the problem caused by the five slow laps behind the official car.

I spent the first lap trying to cope with the car and concentrating on catching Gerhard Berger's Ferrari ahead of me in third place. I could see up ahead that Ayrton was leading Michael and they were quite close. There is no question that Ayrton was highly motivated to beat Michael and I'm sure he was finding it frustrating not to be pulling away during those first few laps.

When I came through Tamburello for the second time, there was dust and debris and a car going sideways across the grass. I could see that it was Ayrton. At the time, I was busy dodging wheels and a nose wing that was flying through the air. I was pretty occupied as I went by but, once I'd got past the scene of the accident, I was concerned for Ayrton's safety. It had obviously been a very big shunt; you don't have a small one on that corner. My initial thoughts were that Ayrton and Michael had tangled and one of them had been pushed off.

LIGHT AND SHADE. HAKKINEN
HAD AN INCIDENT-FREE RACE
AT IMOLA

The race had been stopped and we pulled up at the pit lane entrance. Everyone was asking about what had happened but we had no information. One report suggested Ayrton had been moving. Then they said he was out of the car. But, either way, it was very possible that he was seriously hurt.

Michael explained that Ayrton's car had been bottoming a lot and he'd almost lost it at Tamburello on the previous lap

I was anxious to find out precisely what had taken place. And why. I went over to Michael Schumacher and asked him what he had seen. He explained that Ayrton's car had been bottoming a lot and he'd almost lost it at Tamburello on the previous lap. In his opinion, the same thing had happened again but, this time, Ayrton didn't catch it and went off. I asked Michael if he had seen any hint of trouble, perhaps with the suspension, or the tyres; something like that. He said he hadn't seen any problems at all.

I took all of that on board and made a note to be careful in the early stages when the tyre pressures might be low and perhaps the car is bottoming too much. But I still

AN ALL TOO FAMILIAR VIEW OF
MICHAEL SCHUMACHER

knew nothing about Ayrton's condition. It is one of the less savoury aspects of motor racing that it is not considered to be a good idea to tell the whole truth at the time of an accident in order to get the show over with and send people home none the wiser. Slowly, however, word trickled through that Ayrton's condition was quite serious.

I just couldn't believe that this was happening. I thought that perhaps he'd hurt himself badly and he would be out for a couple of races. That was as much as I knew; that was as much as I would allow myself to think. I tried to concentrate on the race and motivate myself with the thought that it was very important that I get a result for the team. There was nothing I could do about Ayrton. The only thing was to do my job to the best of my ability.

Despite making a reasonable start, that plan was wrecked half-way round the first lap as I tried to take second place off Schumacher. He was trying to get past Gerhard Berger and I don't think he realized I was so close. The Benetton chopped straight across in front of me and accidentally took a nose wing off. That meant a pit stop for a replacement and the task of rejoining at the back of the field. It sounds callous, perhaps, but my thoughts were either, 'Things just aren't going our way this year', or 'My God, this just gets worse'.

Throughout the race, I just kept thinking that this was a job which had to be done. Nothing more than that. Much as I felt like it, there was no way I was going to pull in because that would have been completely the wrong thing to do. The only answer was to try to better the situation the team found themselves in and get the best result I could. Looking at it coldly, it was what I was paid to do and that was about as much enjoyment as I got out of it. One point for sixth place was hardly brilliant. It was something after a climb from last place – but what value was that in the context of everything which had happened over the weekend?

I was pretty shattered by the end of the race. I spoke to Frank and he explained that Ayrton was not in good shape. I just wanted to get away from the circuit; just get in the car and go. Georgie and I could have had a lift in the helicopter if we wanted to wait. But I just wanted to leave as soon as possible.

To learn that Ayrton was dead was like having someone turn off your power supply. I was completely shaken; totally shattered

We did that, even though it meant sitting in a traffic jam for ages. We missed our first flight but I was only worried about how Ayrton was going to pull through all of this. When we reached the airport a member of the team was waiting to tell us that Ayrton was dead.

I had briefly considered that as a possibility but put the thought out of my mind by reflecting on what I had learned about his condition. I had been told that he had serious head injuries and it seemed likely to me that he might never drive again. But that's about as far as my thinking had gone. To learn that he was dead was like having someone turn off your power supply. I was completely shaken; totally shattered.

Georgie and I drove off and stopped at a restaurant where we sat down to think about it all. And you ask yourself over and over again, 'Is it worth it?' That's the bottom line at the end of a weekend like this; always the same question, 'Is it worth it?'

It was not a new sensation for me. I can remember playing in the front room at home when the newsflash came through that Jim Clark had been killed. I knew that he was my Dad's friend and, when my Mum came into the room, I could see she was shocked. I didn't really understand what had happened. But I knew it was bad.

Throughout that period of my life there were occasions when my father had to go to the funerals of friends. It was, without wishing to sound macabre, a gradual introduction to the reality of motor sport, admittedly at a time when the safety standards were nothing like they are now. I remember thinking, 'Hang on, why is Dad doing this? It doesn't make sense.'

And yet he carried on. He did not give up because of the accidents and he drove through what was probably one of the most dangerous periods of Grand Prix racing. The irony was, of course, that he did not actually die in a racing car. And that itself was something which I had to cope with. He raced cars, faced the obvious dangers and yet he died in an aeroplane. Where was the logic in that? It was part of the learning process where I discovered that bad things happen in life, even if you don't put yourself at risk. Horrible things occur all the time.

Bad things happen in life, even if you don't put yourself at risk. Horrible things occur all the time

To me, it seems the real tragedy would be to stop doing something you enjoy. There is no reward without risk. James Hunt died of a heart attack and yet who is to say that he did not live more, cram more into his forty-six years than most people manage in a lifetime? I don't pretend to know the answer.

Probably the easiest thing is to do is carry on and convince yourself that you're doing the right thing. So I forced myself as much as possible to think about giving up and doing something else. Nothing definite sprang to mind but I knew I could do all the things which I had been forced to abandon for the sake of motor racing; weekends off, skiing, more time with the children, see my friends more often; that sort of thing.

And yet I knew that, since an early age, I had always wanted to challenge myself. I needed those punctuations in my life where I had to face up to a severe test and the fact is that few things can offer that sort of opportunity. There are times when I feel totally happy with myself. It may not last long. It might be for a few hours, it could even be for a full day but, quite often, it is only a matter of minutes after I've done something that I'm really proud of. But those moments are addictive. Once you've had one, you need them again and again, like hitting a good golf shot. You subconsciously think of the time when you've had enough (maybe after the highest high) and will give up, completely fulfilled. Until then, you continue to risk all for that fleeting moment.

It may be different for other drivers. In fact, I can't begin to know how people such as Philippe Streiff and Martin Donnelly, put out of racing through serious injury, must feel. How much would they give to get back into a racing car? Or are they simply happy to be alive? It is not the sort of question you can put to them but it is something you need to ask yourself.

There was almost too much time to think about everything during the days which followed. I deliberately chose not to watch television or look at newspapers the following day. I did not see the video of the accident until Tuesday, by which time I had decided that I really ought to find out what had happened. Then I learned that Ayrton's funeral would take place in Sao Paulo.

It was important to show my loyalty as his team-mate. I knew I had to go to the funeral. I'm glad now that I did

The last thing I wanted at that point was to go to Brazil; given the choice, I would have gone away with my family and cut myself off until it was all over. I was not a close friend of Ayrton because I had only really known him for a few months. But the fact was that I had to face certain things: I had to find how and why Ayrton had crashed and it was important to show my loyalty as his team-mate. I knew I had to go to the funeral. I'm glad now that I did.

I discovered just how much Ayrton meant to Brazil. The funeral was almost presidential; quite extraordinary. Thousands of people lined the streets and many ran alongside the cortège. It was a very long way and I saw one person run almost the full distance before falling into a hedge with exhaustion. There was a twenty-one-gun salute carried out with great military precision, a fly-past, a number of dignitaries, including the president of Argentina and the Japanese ambassador.

Ayrton's family had requested that the drivers present escort the coffin as far as they could to the graveside, where there was a rifle salute. Overhead were four or five helicopters; it was a television spectacular of sorts but I couldn't hear any of the service because of the racket from above. I thought it rather sad that the family couldn't be left in peace during those final minutes.

The furore over why he crashed was still raging in the media but, even though I was a member of the team, I was not aware of any animosity. In fact, it seemed to me quite the opposite. I was touched, particularly by the children who would have grown up knowing nothing but the success which Ayrton Senna brought to Brazil. It was obviously very difficult for them to understand what had happened to their hero.

I remember being approached for my autograph by two fans as I left the hotel to go to the funeral. They said that Brazil would be watching me now – and that just choked me with emotion. I suddenly realized that they loved motor racing and, because

NOSE JOB: A SPARE WING AND
NOSE CONE ASSEMBLY

Ayrton had chosen Williams as his team, it had become their team as well. It was not that I was stepping into his Ayrton's shoes or anything like that; it was just that Williams had become a part of their life and, by association, I was a part of it too. I thought it was a truly generous thing for them to say.

All this was a lot for me to take on board. I had been looking forward to racing under the protective umbrella of Ayrton Senna. If I came second to him in a race then I could say I had done a good job – provided he wasn't too far ahead. But suddenly I was discovering the kind of responsibility he had been carrying all these years. He had been expected to win all the time. Being this person Ayrton Senna must have been a burden even if he did choose to carry it in the first place.

In the short time that we had worked together, I had come to understand that he was a pretty special driver, an instinctive driver. If you gave him a car which wasn't quite perfect, he could still make it go very quickly; in fact, I don't think he knew any other way.

I remember being intrigued by the way he would describe how the car handled. He would put his hands up in front of his face as if he was looking through the steering wheel, almost as if he was aiming the car. He had a very, very good ability to recall sensations and talk about the car repeatedly so that the engineer understood exactly what he was trying to say. It was in abstract terms. He wouldn't say the rollbar was too stiff. He would talk about sensations; refer to the road doing this or such and such a corner doing that, things I didn't even consider. He seemed to be able to see in minute detail exactly how the road changed.

If a car was not capable of winning, Ayrton could make it win. In the Brazilian Grand Prix, for instance, he had a car which was a bit off the pace of Schumacher's Benetton. Yet he was able to stay with Michael and I was astounded that he had been able to do that with a car which, if it was anything like mine, simply wasn't handling.

At one stage they were about to lap me. Michael came through and I thought I had better get out of Ayrton's way. But, almost before I had taken the decision, he dived past me and nearly went off. He was heading towards the grass and just managed to slither through. He had completely messed up the corner but, to him, the important thing was to get by; he wasn't going to lose any time hanging around waiting for me.

It was as if he was being sucked towards the end of the race; as if you had attached one end of an elastic band to the start line and wound the rest up for the number of laps – and then just let him go. His desire to win was simply overwhelming. And, judging by the remarkable scenes at his funeral, he was doing it for a nation he loved, a nation which loved him.

CHAPTER SIX
PILING ON THE PRESSURE
THE MONACO GRAND PRIX

THE MONACO GRAND PRIX WAS
SENNA'S MONUMENT, AYRTON
HAVING WON IT MORE TIMES
THAN ANYONE ELSE

f being at Imola was the most unhappy period of my life (after the death of my father), then the weekend at Monaco would prove to be a close second. The pressures and tension associated with racing there make life difficult enough at the best of times, but to have to face all of that just two weeks after Imola meant the annual trip to the Principality was going to be extremely taxing, both mentally and emotionally. To go there as the sole representative of a major team such as Williams, and particularly now that we were without the man who had won at Monaco a record six times, merely piled on more pressure.

Added to this, events in the San Marino Grand Prix had turned the spotlight on to Formula One in a major way. The media was out in force, waiting to jump on the smallest incident and examine it in great detail. The atmosphere, rather than having the usual buzz of excitement, was edgy and, by Monaco's standards, rather sombre.

The repercussions of Imola would continue to dominate everything. The deaths of Roland Ratzenberger and Ayrton Senna had shaken Formula One to the core and everyone was still reeling from the shock while, at the same time, trying their best to bring some form of normality back to the sport as they prepared for this next race.

I held a short and reasonably informal briefing with the press not long after my arrival on Wednesday. I had a feeling of having to suppress and understate my anger and outrage at the lack of safety measures which could have prevented the tragedies of Ayrton and Roland. In order not to feed the hysteria of the hungry press corps, I just said I wished I could be talking about and looking forward to the forthcoming race. But the shadow of Imola continued to loom over us. There was much to be done, many aspects of Formula One which needed to be discussed, and I said I felt, somewhat regrettably, that the race itself would not be the whole story of the weekend.

They were to be prescient words – but not for the reasons I had imagined. I had been referring to the fact that the drivers were going to get together for the first time and discuss their feelings on all matters of safety. What neither I nor anyone else had expected was another disaster on the track.

The morning practice session on the first day, Thursday, was just coming to a close when Karl Wendlinger crashed at the chicane leading on to the harbour front.

At first, there was what amounted to an information blackout; no one was really sure why he had gone off or what the effects had been but, in this already strained atmosphere, the news of another accident simply applied a further turn of the screw.

I was very angry when it finally emerged that he had slammed into the end of a crash barrier protecting a traffic island in the middle of the chicane. I was annoyed because I had pointed out that particular spot earlier in the morning. It was obvious to me that the layout was not right and presented a potential hazard rather than offering some sort of protection. Previously this area had been protected by ample tyres, but now there was only what seemed to me to be insufficient absorbing water-filled plastic barriers.

Just before the chicane, drivers emerge flat out from the tunnel at around 170 mph. Then it is a matter of getting hard on the brakes while running downhill toward

The atmosphere, rather than having the usual buzz of excitement, was edgy and, by Monaco's standards, rather sombre

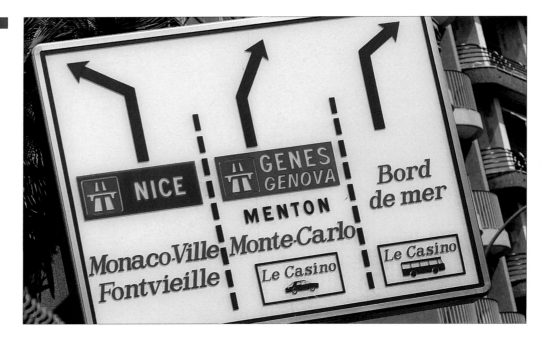

the chicane. It's the fastest approach to any part of the circuit and that's where Wendlinger had lost control of his Sauber.

During practice the previous year, my rear suspension broke just as I came out of the tunnel. I was completely helpless, a passenger as the car went into a spin and three-wheeled its way down the road towards the chicane. I remember bracing myself, waiting to hit something. But, by pure luck, the car curved to the right, instead of travelling straight, and went down the escape road. Apart from brushing the barrier slightly, I didn't actually hit a

The people who approve the layout of circuits don't drive round them at 150 mph

thing. When the car came to a halt, I remember thinking, 'That's it, is it? No big bang? Okay. I'm all right now.' And then I was out of the car and thinking about getting on with practice.

But it was very clear to me this year, when I looked at the same spot, that you were faced with the solid end of a barrier. That is what you aimed at as you came down the hill. The escape road was still there, but you could hardly see it. The danger was perfectly obvious to me and that's why I was doubly annoyed when I discovered that Karl had hit that very same piece of barrier and was in a coma in a Nice hospital.

Max Mosley, the president of the Fédération Internationale du Sport Automobile (FIA), later dismissed this as a freak accident. That really made me angry because a remark like that proved the precise point which the drivers had been trying to get

across. The people who approve the layout of circuits don't drive round them at 150 mph. It looks a lot different then. It really focuses your mind on what might happen if something goes wrong and you hit the pointy bit of metal over here or smash against the sharp edge of a concrete wall over there.

KERB BASHING.
YOU HAVE TO USE ALL THE
ROAD AND MORE FOR A QUICK
LAP AT MONACO

With the best will in the world, officials can't possibly see things as we do while travelling at speed with our backsides an inch or so from the ground. The drivers are only too aware of the dangers, even if they don't – or didn't – always make their views known. Prior to Imola and Monaco, that had been the problem. Drivers were sometimes afraid to voice their opinions for fear of recrimination and appearing to look foolish in isolation.

The sequence of events at Imola had been the catalyst for a meeting in which the drivers would discuss these matters. Indeed, immediately after Roland Ratzenberger's accident, Ayrton had talked of the urgent need for the drivers to get together and speak with one voice. Now, in the wake of Wendlinger's accident, the meeting called for the next day seemed more appropriate than ever.

With the first day's qualifying taking place on the Thursday at Monaco, Friday is free. The drivers gathered in the Automobile Club de Monaco at nine thirty a.m. and we talked for over four hours. We discussed many things, particularly what could be done about the unacceptable dangers on circuits we were due to race on later in the season. It was agreed that we should re-form the Grand Prix Drivers' Association, get together from time to time and have representation within the FIA, the sport's governing body.

I'm not a union man – I don't think any driver likes to be – but it was obvious that unless we put forward our collective view, each driver would continue to get into his car and go racing simply because everyone else was doing it, seemingly without murmur.

In your heart, you might feel a certain aspect of the circuit in question was dangerous but, because everyone else kept quiet about it, so did you. It was a case of exposing yourself to dangers that you might otherwise choose not to. If, for instance, we had all stood up before Imola and said, 'If you're going to go off at Tamburello, you're going to have a big accident and probably get hurt,' then things might have been very different.

The solution to Grand Prix safety is never as simple as it might appear on the outside

When you get the drivers together, there is a consensus. We found that when certain fears were raised – you might be afraid to voice it in public as an individual – other drivers would say: 'I've got that problem too. You're absolutely right! That's the thing which worries me most.'

For instance, everyone felt the cars were getting far too quick again. But, in my case, being fresh into Formula One, I didn't feel it was my place to stand up and say, 'Hey! I'm not driving these cars; they're too dangerous, they're too quick.'

Then you realize that everyone is concerned – but nothing is being said. And that's no good because, by and large, the drivers are the only people at risk and if we don't tackle the issue of safety, then how can we expect anyone else to address the problem?

In the back of every driver's mind was the feeling that there was a basic problem. The FIA recognized that and so did the constructors. But resolving it is the hard part. Any changes you make can be perceived to be in the interests of one team or another and this is the usual sticking point because no one wants to lose what they believe to be an advantage. And that is where the whole issue of Grand Prix safety could fall apart. The solution is never as simple as it might appear on the outside.

That was one of the reasons why we had Niki Lauda on hand to give his experience and insight. He made several valid points about how things were different now compared to the way they had been in the past, particularly with a view to public opinion and the way the sport is received in living rooms around the world. It was a pretty serious meeting and we were determined to come out of it looking professional, as opposed to emotional.

Of course, all of this – worthwhile though it may have been – was another distraction. It was easy to forget that I had come to Monaco to try to win the Grand Prix. To be honest, I had not spent much time thinking about the race during the previous two weeks. Having been to Brazil for Ayrton's funeral, I was pretty tired after such an emotionally draining experience. Overall, little time had been spent on considering how the car should be set up and I was as much to blame for that as anyone. But it could not be denied that this necessary diversion was a factor in finding that the car was far from right when I went out for the first time. And I can't deny that there was always the thought of just how easy it would be to end up like Karl – or even Ayrton.

FW16 had been a difficult car from the word go but we had started to get on top of it. And then we found that we were right off the pace at

I can't deny that there was always the thought of just how easy it would be to end up like Karl — or even Ayrton

Monaco – and I didn't have any back-up from a team-mate. Again, this was yet more pressure because the bottom line was that I wanted to do a good solid job. I could see that everyone needed it. But, as I said earlier, Monaco is the last place to be thrown into a situation such as this.

It was a great pity because, in many ways, it is such a tremendous event. If you ask people with no interest in the sport to name a motor race they would probably say Le Mans, maybe Indianapolis and most certainly, Monaco. It embodies the essence of Formula One as people feel it ought to be – fast cars, glamour, glitzy surroundings, playboy haven, that sort of thing.

This race attracts more attention than any other and everyone seems to behave a little differently as a result. Certainly, there are black tie dinners and sponsors' parties. But you meet people who have absolutely no interest in Formula One and yet they come along simply because it's the place to be. It is fun although, at the same time, it is also quite shallow.

For the people who have to actually work in the pits, it's hell. The pit lane was never meant to be used in this way simply because it is part of a normal promenade for fifty-one weeks of the year. The paddock itself is some distance away on the quayside and moving back and forth between practice sessions is quite an ordeal.

Then there is the noise. It's incessant and very loud, even by the standards we are accustomed to. There is no way of escaping it because the sound of the cars echoes through the streets, bounces off the buildings and the cliff face and comes at

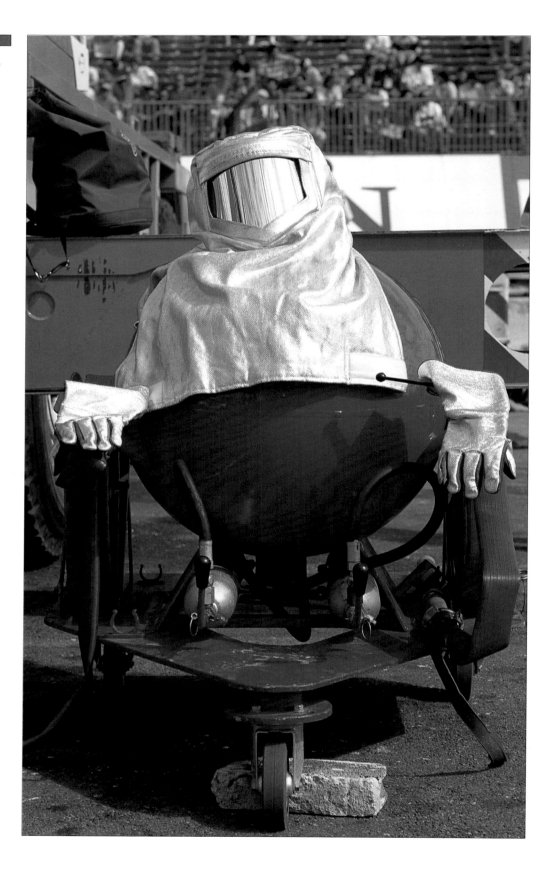

THE MONACO GRAND PRIX

you from all directions. It is necessary to shout and this wears your nerves down a bit.

But, having said that, there is nowhere better when it comes to being impressed by Formula One cars in action. The circuit provides a unique mixture of sensations. The hairpin outside the Loews Hotel, for instance, is the slowest place on any race track in the world. It seems as though the cars are only doing 20 mph and the engines don't make any noise because drivers can't touch the throttle until the car is safely pointing out of the corner. All you can hear is the sound of bits of bodywork scraping the ground. And yet, just a few yards up the road, the cars have been through Casino Square, flat out at 150 mph and getting sideways on the adverse camber. Watch there for just a few seconds and it makes your hair stand on end!

Nelson Piquet once compared Monaco with trying to ride a bicycle around your living room

It's an impressive sight and, I can assure you, it feels equally awe-inspiring in the cars. There have been all sorts of metaphors to describe the sensation which comes with trying to tame a 700 bhp Formula One car in such tight confines. Nelson Piquet once compared it with trying to ride a bicycle around your living room. Someone else likened it to a bullet whistling down the barrel of a rifle as you travel between the triple layers of barrier which appear to close in from either edge of the road.

The trouble is, there is absolutely no room for error – yours or anyone else's. Passing slower cars during qualifying or the race can provide an extremely anxious moment or two. You hope they've seen you coming and will move over. But you don't really know until it is too late. The last thing you want is to touch wheels with someone at a place like Monaco.

Your heart really races here. You actually get exhausted by the strain on your nerves, more so than at other circuits. It is also truly great fun – you wouldn't subject yourself to such an ordeal if it wasn't – but I can't think of any other circuit which brings such an awareness of the need to overcome fear.

The paradox is that elsewhere, the sensation of speed is not so great as at Monaco because the cars are driven much further away from the crash barriers. The only occasion you would see them closely is when you fly off the road – which, in itself, is cause enough to instil plenty of fear.

But, at Monaco, it does not take much imagination to realize that it would hurt if you slammed into the steel walls waiting to penalize the slightest mistake. And if it is

RACE MARSHALS PAY TRIBUTE TO
AYRTON SENNA

not rows of tiered metal towering above you, then it is permanent hazards such as kerbs and concrete walls sweeping quickly into view.

Down by the entry to the swimming pool chicane, for example, you have the worst of both worlds with a wall on one side and a bit of barrier and another wall on the other. And the entry is completely blind. You go through every kind of emotion in a fraction of a second; anger, relief, fear, excitement, annoyance, self-belief, lack of self-belief! The turmoil we drivers go through!

Initially, you are concerned about the left-hand wall. The car is bouncing around but it's not a case of choosing a smooth line through the left-right, it's a case of hitting a bump at the precise moment so that the car doesn't bounce sideways and throw you into the right-hand wall at the exit. This is all done at something like 130 mph and the instant you sneak through and see the road at the exit, there is momentary relief as you go hard on the throttle again – but only for a fraction of a second because there is another tight corner coming up.

SCHUMACHER ROUNDS

LOEWS HAIRPIN, MONACO'S

TIGHTEST CORNER

And so it goes on, corner after corner. Even the straight – so-called – climbing up the hill is an awesome place because the road curves and turns and, when you reach the top, you can't see what's over the crest. You arrive flat out. Barrier on either side, of course. Then it is a very short piece of straight and another corner, quite a quick left-hander this time.

That is the unique feature of Monaco. You are always cornering, always having to concentrate on positioning the car. It does things to your mind. After a while, you get into a trance-like state. You find yourself asking, 'Am I driving this car – or is it doing it all by itself?' It is completely different to anything else; very interesting in its own peculiar way.

People say racing there requires a special knack and, when the conversation moves into that area, my father's name always crops up. He won the Monaco Grand Prix five times and I suppose it was natural that the press should latch on to this when I raced at Monaco for the first time in 1993, the year Ayrton finally broke my father's

record. Even so, I was surprised by the strength of some of the stories. It almost became an obsession with some journalists and I couldn't really agree with that. After all, it was eighteen years since my father had died and he last won the race in 1969. And yet a lot of people seemed to think that it would almost be a natural progression; that I should come to Monaco and win.

My father's success is part of racing legend and I'm very proud of his reputation there. But I'm also wary of trying to poach a part of it. It would have made a great story if I had won Monaco, so I consciously fended off sentimental predictions and tried to be as realistic as possible. But, having said that, I was very, very proud to walk up to the rostrum in 1993 and collect my trophy for finishing second. I'd seen it so many times, the pictures of my father in the royal box, and I was very aware of the significance of my presence when I made my way up those steps. It was a terrific feeling.

I remember thinking, during the race itself, that if Senna broke down, then I'd win at Monaco on my first visit. But he didn't retire and it reminded me of how things just don't happen like that. It is worth shooting for, of course, but there's no magic at all. In fact, if I'd won, I think I would have retired on the spot because there is no way I could ever equal a dream result like that!

I must admit, such flippant thoughts were far from my mind twelve months later. As I said earlier, the car was still not close enough to perfect. It danced around a little too much for my liking. Dancing at Monaco should be confined to the Hotel de Paris and strictly forbidden in Casino Square. But a lot of careful thought and analysis had us in better shape for final qualifying. I managed to set fourth fastest time and felt I was doing a good job because the car was still quite difficult. It was disappointing not to be on the front row at Monaco since that is one of the few ways you can help guarantee a trouble-free race but, nevertheless, I still felt that, all things considered, the second row of the grid was quite respectable.

FAMILY HISTORY. THE NAME MAY HAVE CHANGED FROM 'STATION HAIRPIN' TO 'LOEWS HAIRPIN' BUT THIS PIECE OF TRACK REMAINS EXACTLY AS IT WAS WHEN MY FATHER RACED AT MONACO

My father's success at Monaco is part of racing legend and I'm very proud of his reputation

On the morning of the race, we changed the car again and it really felt good during the warm-up. So, now I had come from a very anxious and slightly fraught start to the weekend, to being much more confident with the car and really looking forward to the race. As you walk from the paddock to the pits, the crowds are stacked high on the rock face to the left and packed into a grandstand on the right. There were a lot of Union Jacks to be seen and plenty of people cheering. It was extremely heartening; I really wanted to get stuck into this race because I now felt I could do whatever was asked of me.

Just before the start, all the drivers gathered at the front of the grid (the first row had actually been left vacant in memory of Roland and Ayrton) to show their respect. We knew it would be a difficult moment just before the start, particularly at Monaco, but I know that all the drivers felt that this was an entirely correct thing to do. It also showed a GPDA united in respect. Some drivers were a bit emotional, and that was to be expected. Personally, I thought making this small gesture was a very good thing.

MARTIN BRUNDLE SWINGS ON TO
THE HARBOUR-FRONT

SCHUMACHER HAS NO TIME
FOR SHOPPING AS HE RUSHES
TOWARDS CASINO SQUARE

Having been to Ayrton's funeral, I found that it does help to exorcise all those feelings of loss and grief and I think that makes things easier in the long run. I know, once we dispersed, I was absolutely ready for a good race. And I knew that was exactly how Ayrton and Roland would have wanted us to feel. Quite what they would have made of the next bit, I'm not so sure.

I made an absolutely brilliant start. Mika Hakkinen (second fastest to Schumacher during practice and therefore directly in front of me on the grid) had moved to the right to block Berger. Mika was now on the inside line for the corner and I was closing in on him. That would have been fine if Hakkinen had stayed where he was.

My momentum was so good that I got to the point where I was actually starting to pull alongside the McLaren as we headed towards the first corner. I started to drop back – got on the brakes – because I knew I couldn't actually overtake him. The intention was to slot in behind the McLaren. But then he started to move back across to his left. I was now hard on the brakes and heading towards the barrier.

I thought, 'If I'm lucky, he's just going to knock me.' But he hit me quite hard. He spun off and I tried to get round the corner and carry on even though my steering was broken. Monaco is a long race and you never know. I remember my father won on one occasion after spinning down the escape road to avoid a slower car, stalling his engine and then getting out to give the BRM a push-start! In my case, it might have been feasible to fix the track rod and, even if I was two laps down, it might still have been possible to get a point. I badly wanted to race; I really wanted to do well.

There is nothing worse than having a race going on around you — and you're not in it

I got as far as Casino Square and the other track rod broke, leaving me with no steering at all. There was no option but to pull over to one side and park. I climbed out and a crane lifted my car out of harm's way. I sat for a while and stared dejectedly at the nearby flowerbeds, going over and over those fateful first few 100 metres in my mind. Cars were blasting past and I just could not believe what had happened. It was very difficult to take. But I knew the damage to the morale of the team would be equal to mine.

This was the worst possible example of what can happen when a team runs just one car. There is always some consolation when you've got two cars but, on this occasion, it was all or nothing. And we had nothing in less than a minute. I walked back to the pits and the sight of the team packing up while the race was only a few laps old really brought it home. There is nothing worse than having a race going on around you — and you're not in it.

It would have been terrific if we had finished in the top three; just marvellous. But it didn't happen. It had been a desperately long weekend. I have never been so glad to get out of a place that has so many happy memories for the Hill family.

CHAPTER SEVEN

DIFFICULT RECOVERY

THE SPANISH AND CANADIAN GRANDS PRIX

SAFETY ON PARADE

Safety has to be on every motor racing agenda these days. Forty years ago, it was considered almost an irrelevance. The risks attached to racing in the 1950s were thought to be mild when compared with the terrible perils forced upon people fighting in a war which had ended less than a decade before. Now, we are acutely aware of the danger and that realization had been heightened this year by events leading up to the Monaco Grand Prix. It was hardly surprising that there was no respite during the period between the races in Monte Carlo and Barcelona; whichever way you turned, the subject of safety, and what to do about it, kept leaping to prominence.

The sport's governing body, the FIA, had introduced a series of reforms designed to slow the cars and the first of those changes was coming into force in time for the Spanish Grand Prix. The profile of the front wings had been altered and a large portion of the rear undertray – the diffuser – had to be chopped off. This reduced downforce and therefore the amount of grip available. It meant a fairly major change to the way the car performed.

We had a pretty torrid time trying to find a decent balance on the latest car during a test session at Jerez and I left the road once or twice. But, as we headed north to Barcelona, I was quite confident that we were coming to terms with the car. That was important, because the team needed to re-establish itself. And quickly.

We arrived at the Circuit de Catalunya and I was immediately involved in a four-hour Grand Prix Drivers' Association meeting about safety at the track. We agreed that a chicane should be installed and, at nine o'clock that night, Niki Lauda, our spokesperson, was trying to contact Max Mosley. He probably choked on his paella when told that the drivers would boycott the meeting unless a tyre chicane was approved by the FIA before the morning! That done, we returned to the circuit, ready to start practice on Friday morning, only to discover that several team owners were having a meeting — and their cars would not be running. Williams was among them.

There is an argument which predicates that, as safety increases, the risks drivers take also increase

The teams were expressing concern about the integrity of the cars, saying that there had been insufficient time to test them thoroughly in the latest guise. In fact, there was a political overtone to all of this, arising from the continual power struggle between the constructors (FOCA) and the organizers. But it was typical of the mood that safety should be a prime concern.

It is important to put the safety argument in context. Safety in all aspects of life has become a serious topic for discussion only during the past fifteen or twenty years. Before that, for instance, it used to be acceptable to drink and drive. People had come through the Second World War when they did the most extraordinarily brave things, not through choice but purely for survival. So driving a racing car was bound to be a lot less dangerous – relatively speaking – and also more enjoyable when compared to going on a low-level bombing raid, or whatever.

Looking back at motor racing in the 1950s, drivers were willingly putting themselves at incredible risk – almost for enjoyment's sake – by doing things that would have been considered run of the mill only ten years earlier. In Formula One, they were going

'OW! THAT BLOODY HURTS!'
JOSEF GIVES DAMON THE
TREATMENT IN SPAIN

racing, having a good time and getting paid for it. To mention the fact that it was dangerous, to talk about things such as seat belts, would have been considered absurd. They drove quite happily with cardboard crash helmets and in short-sleeved shirts.

It was not until the mid-1960s that motor racing started to take the subject seriously. Drivers began to appreciate that, if they wore flameproof gear from head to foot, they might stand a better chance of saving themselves from the serious and often fatal burns which were commonplace at the time. Seat harnesses and proper full-face crash helmets became part of the accepted kit. Now we have on-board fire extin-

guishers, survival cells, full medical back-up. It has been a slow process, but a worthwhile one.

Of course, there is a downside to everything. There is an argument which predicates that, as safety increases, the risks drivers take also increase. It is the converse of the theory about having a spike on the steering wheel, the assumption being that if drivers are confronted with a spike pointing towards them, they automatically use more caution and are therefore involved in fewer accidents. But, obviously, this is not a serious suggestion, merely a way of countering the argument for improved safety.

It has reached the point where drivers began to regard the risk as a minor one and drove accordingly

However, the connection with Formula One is clear. It has become commonplace to see people walk away from accidents which logic tells you should have put them in hospital at the very least. It has reached the point where drivers began to regard the risk as a minor one and drove accordingly, taking dangerous chances on the track. Imola changed all that. It was a harsh reminder that drivers could get killed, something which had been an inevitable and terrible part of the sport right up to the early 1970s.

Drivers such as Jackie Stewart and my father were going to funerals all too regularly. It was clear that something had to be done and they went out of their way to make things happen. They put steel barriers, run-off areas, catch-fencing, gravel traps and seat belts on the safety agenda and they pursued this cause until racing became much safer. Fewer people were getting hurt and the process continued until we had a run of twelve years without a fatality in a Grand Prix. We got to the stage where drivers didn't think about safety any more; or, at least, they didn't think about it as much as they should.

Now, of course, putting on protective clothing is a matter of routine. My overalls offer a certain amount of security and I wear a flameproof vest underneath. I choose not to wear leggings because that's the area which is least likely to get burnt. That may seem cavalier but you have to weigh up the fact that you are sitting in very cramped surroundings and it gets extremely sweaty. You lose a lot of fluid during a race so it is necessary to think very hard about the amount of clothing you put on.

The risk of fire is always there but I think we've reduced the amount we're prepared to do to protect ourselves simply because the chances of it happening are a lot less. For instance, we all know that if a plane crashes, you could easily have quite a big fire. Yet they don't put fire-fighting equipment on board. We don't think twice about that apparent shortcoming although I'm sure anyone unlucky enough to have been on a plane which had caught fire might take a different view.

Patrick Head and his engineers put a lot of store into making their cars safe

In racing, as in flying, you could take things to the extreme, to the point where it starts to get silly, like wearing asbestos suits. It is always a question of how much of a risk you are prepared to take. Drivers don't want to dwell on that sort of thing. I think most of us take the view that you can't decide against doing things simply because there is a risk involved. Generally speaking, it is usually more worthwhile doing something which involves a risk of some sort. That's part of the philosophy. The only difference is that, when you are young, you are less aware of the risks and sometimes do crazy things as a result. The older you get, there is no question you become more conscious of the potential hazards.

In April, I took one or two MPs for a couple of laps round Silverstone. They may not, in their heart of hearts, have wanted to do it – I don't know. But they weighed everything up and took the decision to get in the car. They probably reckoned I knew what I was doing and, at the same time, they got a thrill from the fact that they were scared, the feeling that there was always the chance that it might not work out.

Whether they admit it or not, people are always thinking about the potential for things to go horribly wrong. But they put that to the back of their minds – and do whatever it is anyway. They feel great afterwards about having got the better of fear. Nobody wants to be oppressed by it; nobody wants to be handicapped and prevented from ultimately having enjoyment. That's what it's all about.

Once you have taken the decision to commit yourself to go racing, you can't honestly claim to be surprised by the potential which exists to have an accident. But you

NEW TEAM-MATE ENJOYS OLD
JOKE. DAVID COULTHARD AND HIS
ENGINEER, DAVID BROWN

can do your best to make sure that mistakes, as far as possible, are eradicated from your driving because it will make you a better driver and, in any case, you can't afford the risk. You also have to put your faith in the engineering integrity of the car and driving for someone like Williams makes that a comforting thought. Patrick Head and his engineers put a lot of store into making their cars safe; they won't take silly risks and that does your confidence a lot of good.

Drivers tend to stick their necks out more during qualifying. You're never sure if it's possible but you know it's worth trying to see if the move comes off. You gamble more at that stage in the weekend. In a race, you are aware that getting to the finish is of paramount importance and you can't afford to speculate so wholeheartedly – unless, of course, it's an all-or-nothing race on which the championship depends. In a way, that's a relief because you know you don't have to be conservative.

If it's a race in which finishing either second or third won't make that much difference in the short term – but it could be very important in the long run – then I am

The rivalry between Renault and Peugeot was more intense than ever and added yet another dimension to the pressure

slightly less prepared to make the complete commitment and risk not finishing. Alain Prost was accused of not taking many risks but he gambled enough to get the equation right and win more races than anyone else. I think it is accepted that Ayrton Senna took more risks than Alain Prost, and Nigel Mansell might have won more championships if he had avoided taking gambles which didn't pay off. Some drivers are very much admired because of their daring – but, usually, they're not very successful. Gilles Villeneuve, for instance, was one of the sport's biggest risk takers and he might have been even more victorious if he had managed to level out his ability. But then he wouldn't have been Gilles Villeneuve. It depends on your philosophy and how you want to approach your racing.

The risk-taking aspect was more or less taken out of the drivers' hands during what should have been the first practice session for the Spanish Grand Prix. The majority of team managers were holding a discussion over the rule changes I mentioned at the beginning of the chapter and it meant that most of the cars stayed in the garages.

I wasn't too concerned because I knew the circuit and it was obvious that the serious competition – in other words, Michael Schumacher – would suffer from the same handicap. But it was much worse for my new team-mate, David Coulthard. This was to be his first Grand Prix and, even though he was our test driver, he hadn't actually driven FW16 before. It meant the first time he would drive the car in earnest would be when he had to go out and qualify. Formula One can be tough!

So, it was a matter of making an educated guess with the settings on the car and

then launching straight in. The FW16 was a bit tricky to drive but, even though I was third quickest, I had expected to do better despite the limited amount of time on the track. But the same applied to Michael Schumacher – on provisional pole with the Benetton – and Mika Hakkinen, whose second fastest time with the McLaren-Peugeot was merely turning up the heat on Williams-Renault.

BARCELONA

THE GPDA CHICANE.

A NERVE-WRACKING OBSTACLE

The rivalry between Renault and Peugeot, particularly after my early retirement and McLaren's second place at Monaco, was more intense than ever and added yet another dimension to the pressure on a team which had lost its Number One driver and was looking to me to produce the results. David Coulthard was inexperienced and they couldn't expect him to do all the work. It meant that the need to succeed was building all the time; something had to be done about the situation which had been thrust upon us at Imola.

The way I coped was to get pretty aggressive about it all. I reminded myself that I hadn't asked to be put under this kind of pressure; I can only do my best and that's all there is to it. And yet you only had to look at some of the faces in the team to see what was going through their minds. They were extremely worried about whether or not we were going to pull through and I knew that such open concern in certain quarters was merely the tip of an underlying unease for everyone else. In the face of all of that, it was an immense relief finally to qualify on the front row. Even if I say so myself, I did what I considered to be a bloody good job with a car which was still far from right.

But the remedy was only temporary. During the warm-up on race morning, I spun off and that brought some of the tension back again. I was hacked off about dumping the car in the sand and, needless to say, it didn't go down too well with certain people. Then the spare car developed a problem which meant I could not run at all.

We were back to square one again. Everything had been turned on its head. It was high pressure once more as everyone wondered what particular fate was going to befall us in this race. The single most important thing was to get a result. It was vital to be among the points-scorers. Another retirement would have been too much to take.

A driver knows that the easiest thing to change about a car, if it is not going well, is the driver. I was determined this should not happen to me

On the evidence of practice, it was unlikely that we would be able to beat Schumacher and Benetton in a straight fight. But I thought there was still a chance. Much would depend on strategy. If he was going to make three stops, then we might be in good shape because our car was good for just two pit stops, and that would gain time over the Benetton.

I was more focused for the start of that race than I had been for some time. I knew exactly what I had to achieve. But I can't say I was particularly happy. I believed strongly that I was doing a good job under difficult circumstances, but I also felt increasingly uncomfortable because I didn't get the impression that it was generally appreciated how tough a car the FW16 was to set up. Consequently, I thought my driving ability would be drawn into question as the obvious target for blame.

This could be called 'Sportsperson's Paranoia' but a driver knows that the easiest thing to change about a car, if it is not going well, is the driver. I was determined this should not happen to me. However, it did not stop me having moments of serious situation assessment. Several times that weekend I reached the point where I started to think negatively. The pressure was so great that it was beginning to strain relationships within the team. It was a fairly unpleasant environment. Frank gave me a lot of encouragement by saying he felt I was capable of delivering what he wanted. But I was never sure whether he was saying that simply to get out of me the performance the team needed, or whether he truly meant it. Driver's paranoia?

I don't necessarily need to be mollycoddled. In fact, the more hacked off I am, the better I go. But it is important that the team is behind their driver. I certainly don't need someone telling me that things are going wrong when I can see that for myself. I felt that Patrick, for example, was not at all happy with my occasional spins and wasted little time in letting me know that the Williams Grand Prix team expected higher standards

from their drivers. However, it was necessary to remember that he was also under a lot of stress – as was the entire team. It was not a happy place at the time. Everyone wanted a result to be proud of so badly that it was cramping our style.

Things had changed in many ways. The previous year, I always had the fallback of knowing I was just one part of the package. I had always felt that the results I achieved were only really of importance to me. Now I was being made aware that the results were of immense importance to a lot of people – and I was the guy in the car. I felt uncomfortable about that because I reckoned I was still learning. After all, I was only halfway through my second season and suddenly all of this had happened. But nobody had any time to consider that. This is Formula One – ready or not.

My state of mind before the race was something like, 'Well, stuff you lot. I'm going to do what I'm going to do, and we'll see what happens.' Once again, I couldn't afford to make a mistake in the first few laps. I had to be very cautious and Michael was building up quite a good lead. That was to be expected and I had to balance the thought of attacking his advantage with an overwhelming need to get a good finish. This was not a case of pushing hard, knowing I'd got nothing to lose. The fact was I had too much to lose. I was forced into driving the best race I could, but with minimum risk. Second place was going to have to do on this occasion, much as it hurts to admit it.

You can imagine my excitement when Michael ran into difficulties and I suddenly caught and passed him; there wasn't a great deal of sympathy coming from my direction. My main thought was that it was about time he had a bit of bad luck. So much for sportsmanship! After that, I felt this race was going to be between Mika and me. I knew we had the edge on McLaren and if I played it sensibly, the Spanish Grand Prix could be in the bag for Williams.

To my great surprise, Michael didn't drop out completely. But I felt comfortable that we had the right strategy for the race. And yet, even though everything was under control from quite early on, I didn't let myself think about it. In fact, I was driving, not so much instinctively, but with a conscious effort. It was like having someone

Although Benetton had bad luck, I reckoned the result was vindication of the way I had been going about my job

in the car with you; similar to doing the driving test when you know the person sitting alongside is watching every move. You don't relax and everything seems clumsy. It's not natural.

Looking back on it now, it is obvious that failing to finish the Spanish Grand Prix would have been a complete disaster. But I never thought about that for a second during the actual race. I was going to bring the car home in the points, come what may. If Michael had stayed ahead of me, I would have tried to catch him but, even though this may sound like sacrilege, I wasn't going to throw absolutely everything into trying to win; that's how vital it was for me on this occasion to simply bring the car home in the highest position I could.

I was concentrating so hard that when I turned the last corner and knew all I had to do was accelerate to the line, it was a brilliant feeling. Until that moment, I had not allowed myself to think that a much-needed victory was there for the taking. The relief was indescribable. It was almost like winning a Grand Prix for the first time; I felt a hurdle had been overcome. It was the breakthrough we needed and, although Benetton had bad luck, I reckoned the result was vindication of the way I had been going about my job.

This was the first time Schumacher had been beaten all season. More than that, it was the first time Williams and Renault had won a race since my victory at Monza

the previous September. It was also the first-ever Formula One victory for our sponsor, Rothmans, and the 300th win for Goodyear! I felt we had turned the tide of events which had been flowing against us. Schumacher had finished second and no one could claim we had beaten Benetton in a straight fight but, nevertheless, we had been granted an opportunity to generate some positive feeling within the team. It was the first good thing to have happened for what seemed like months and months and I was determined to take maximum advantage from this.

On the slowing down lap, a marshal came forward and handed me a Union Jack which someone in the crowd must have given him. I was delighted to carry it high on my way back to the pits – but there's no pleasing some people. The next day, a bloke wrote to the *Daily Telegraph* and complained about my disgraceful behaviour.

The victory was the first good thing to have happened for what seemed like months and months

He said I should be ashamed of myself for waving a Union Jack which was upside down! Maybe it was. There was no disrespect intended. I was simply thrilled to have the chance to express, in any way I could, the wonderful sense of freedom which came with that victory.

I felt the time was right to stand up and be counted. It so happened that rumours were gathering force concerning a possible Formula One comeback by Nigel Mansell and I took the conscious decision to blow my own trumpet and say, 'Hey! You haven't finished with me.' Or, more to the point, 'I haven't finished with you!' I was at a function in London for the Down's Syndrome Association and I took the opportunity to give some off-the-cuff remarks to a couple of reporters who had turned up. I thought it was a chance to remind people that I was quite capable of doing the job as Number One, provided Williams and Renault were prepared to support me. And I could say it with conviction, having come through such a torrid six weeks and then scored the victory in Spain.

That's all very well but, in this business, you are only as good as your last win. When we got to Montreal two weeks later, this was a new race, a different challenge. Barcelona may as well never have happened. It was back to square one yet again.

You are constantly having to prove yourself in Formula One. That brings out the best and the worst in people at difficult times and it makes you look very hard at what you are doing. You question whether or not you are going about things in the right way and whether any criticism fired in your direction is valid. As in most things, it's a little bit of both and, although it may seem an acrimonious situation at the time, in actual

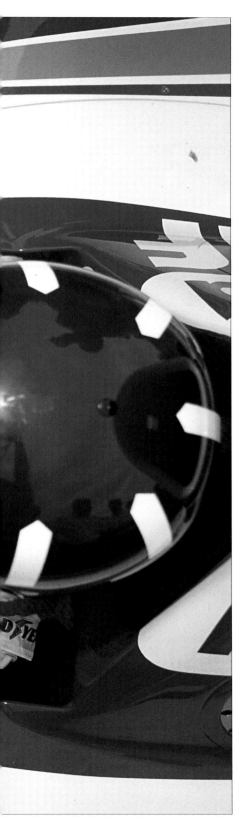

fact, it is probably therapeutic and cathartic.

My attitude was pretty much, 'Well, I've got confidence in what I'm doing, so let's just press on.' The stories about Mansell didn't make much difference either way. Once practice began for the Canadian Grand Prix, I was only concerned about making the car better and beating Michael. I was determined to enjoy it and have a good time; a case of devil take the hindmost.

In the end, I had to take fourth place on the grid. I felt I had driven well but we were still off the pace when it came to finding the best set-up for the car. David Coulthard and I had gone in different directions and I wasn't sure which was the better of the two solutions. Certainly, it was very close, David qualifying in fifth place for his second Grand Prix and I was just a fraction slower than Gerhard Berger's Ferrari. The Circuit Gilles Villeneuve – complete with a new chicane to slow the cars for a previously daunting series of 170 mph swerves with no run-off area whatsoever – suited the powerful Ferrari V12 perfectly and Jean Alesi was second fastest. Almost inevitably, Schumacher was on pole – but this time, he'd been forced to work very hard.

I was under no illusions about what Benetton were capable of in the race. But I thought, one way or another, the Ferraris would not be so competitive. They would have either fuel or tyre trouble and second place seemed a strong possibility for Williams – with the optimistic thought that Schumacher's reliability might be suspect again.

My attitude was pretty much, 'Well, I've got confidence in what I'm doing, so let's just press on.'

ALL AFTER THE SAME PIECE
OF ROAD

I also had to consider David. I knew he was very keen to make an impression and yet I was in the position of wanting to close the points gap on Schumacher. Logically, it would have been right to have team orders because there were, at that stage, eleven races to go and everything should have been done to help keep the points deficit to a minimum. However, nothing was said by the team management before the race. I had a word with David and pointed out that we should be careful through the first corner. He agreed with that but it was clear that he was out to race and, quite honestly, I wouldn't have expected anything less of any team-mate under these circumstances.

The question of the first corner resolved itself when I made a dreadful start and David got through on the inside. We were fourth and fifth, with David right on Berger's tail. It soon became clear that we were not going to get much further and I could see Schumacher and Alesi pulling away, but not as dramatically as I thought might be the case.

After a couple of laps, I could see that David was not going to get past Berger, so I tried a couple of manoeuvres when my team-mate made one or two mistakes. David was pretty defensive and, while you can't blame him for that, it might have occurred to him that, if he was not getting away from me and I was trying to overtake, then perhaps he ought to give some thought to letting me through to have a go at Berger.

I fully understood that he wanted to make a name for himself. But I didn't approve of his tactics. I got on the radio and suggested it might be a good idea if David did something other than hold me up. To be fair to him, as soon as he was instructed to move over, he let me through. I set after Gerhard and caught him quite quickly. The car was handling reasonably well and it was a very good feeling to be making progress. I was really enjoying this and I felt even better when Berger made an error and gave me the chance to get alongside and take third place.

My momentum was hardly disrupted and I chased after Alesi, getting to within a couple of seconds of the Ferrari before his pit stop. I knew I was due to come in two laps later and I used that time to really push hard and make up as much advantage as I could. On top of which, the team did an excellent job adding fuel and changing tyres – I didn't help by almost breaking a mechanic's arm when I engaged gear before the car was off its jacks and he had not finished tightening one of the rear wheel nuts – and I rejoined just ahead of Alesi.

You could argue that it was not terribly exciting in terms of actual racing. But I have to admit that was the least of my concerns; I was ahead of Alesi and no longer had the problem of trying to overtake a car with very impressive acceleration.

But what about Schumacher? He was 55 seconds in the lead and, for a while, it

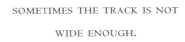

SOMETIMES THE TRACK IS NOT
WIDE ENOUGH.
DAVID COULTHARD GIVES ME THE
SQUEEZE. AT TIMES LIKE THIS,
CAMARADERIE IS NOT A FACTOR

DON'T FENCE ME IN

began to look as if he was not going to stop at all. If that was the case, then he had started the race with at least 200 litres of fuel and could run at a pace which matched the best we could do with half the amount of fuel on board. It was a depressing thought.

Michael did stop eventually – comparatively late in the race – but that did not lessen the fact that Benetton could do more or less as they pleased: stop early, stop late; carry very little fuel, carry plenty of fuel. It didn't really make much difference. It made you wonder how on earth they managed to dominate so convincingly. Indeed, I should add at this point that there had been some criticism of the Benetton and its ability to put

the power down without any wheelspin. Somehow Benetton appeared to be doing something different to avoid the kind of wheelspin which was affecting the rest of us. But, while there was a lot of muttering in the paddock, no one had actually come out and said anything.

Schumacher rejoined about 30 seconds ahead of me and I drew some consolation from the fact that he was not pulling away. I was convinced he was running as hard as I was because the gap between us remained constant. If he had been cruising, then I would have expected to see him suddenly go a second a lap quicker every now and again, just to see what he could do and to keep me in my place. With about fifteen laps to go, it became apparent I wasn't going to make much impression on him. All I could hope was that something would happen to him – nothing serious, but it would have to be something like a complete gearbox failure since Spain had proved that leaving him with just one gear was not enough.

Somehow Benetton appeared to be doing something different to avoid the kind of wheelspin which was affecting the rest of us

It served me right to entertain such mildly flippant thoughts when I began to have a novel and desperately serious problem of my own. For some reason, I felt as though I was choking. It was as if someone had their hands around my throat and the grip was getting tighter and tighter. I pulled off the pipe feeding the drink supply to my helmet, but that made no difference. The sensation was getting worse and worse. I began to wonder if something had come off the track, got itself wrapped around my neck, was trailing behind the car and was on the point of getting caught in a rear wheel. I hadn't a clue what it was. And still it got tighter. I was at panic stations by this stage, so much so that the thought of not scoring any points had become secondary. That's how bad it was.

DESPITE THE TIGHT TRACK,
CANADA HAS A FEELING OF SPACE

I detached my radio flex from the helmet and undid my overalls. After a couple of laps the problem began to clear itself and I can only assume that the bouncing and jarring dished out by this circuit had worked either my overalls or my flameproof vest down my back, pulling the neckline across my throat in the process.

Then, with about three laps to go, the car nearly ran out of petrol. It coughed as I came through one of the chicanes. This was just about the last straw. My heart was in my mouth for the next five minutes or so and, as I completed the final slowing down lap, the engine died as I headed down the pit lane towards parc ferme at the far end.

The car actually stopped right outside the Williams garage and there was immediate panic because the pit lane was being invaded by spectators at the same time. The rules say that, on pain of disqualification, no one must touch the car until it reaches final

BLANKET COVERAGE. THE TYRES
GET THE HEAT TREATMENT TO
ENSURE OPTIMUM TEMPERATURE
AND MAXIMUM PERFORMANCE

scrutineering. Dickie Stanford, the chief mechanic, was struggling to keep people away from the car while shouting at the mechanics not to touch it. I'm afraid I was so relieved that I just sat there with a big grin and my thumbs up as if to say, thanks for getting me this far; I really didn't think I'd make it to the finish.

I reckoned I had done a solid job by taking on and beating both Ferraris. Second place behind the flying Benetton was just about as much as we could have hoped for.

Second place behind the flying Benetton was about as much as we could have hoped for

Inevitably, because the race had been a bit boring in the latter stages and there wasn't much to write about, someone at the press conference raised the business of being held up by my team-mate. I didn't want to be drawn on the subject but I said I was a bit cheesed off and I intended to have a word with David. And that's what I did eventually. I felt it was better to get it off my chest, let him know immediately and then start afresh. Of course, the newspapers the following day put a bit of topspin on the whole thing and I regretted that. I began to wish I had never said anything because I thought I had come out of it badly. I don't like animosity; I don't like having bad feelings. But, at the same time, something had to be done and I felt I was right to make the point.

All told, it was an unfortunate way to end a weekend which I had really enjoyed. We were making progress with the car and I actually felt better about this race than I had about winning in Spain. The Spanish Grand Prix had been about overcoming a huge psychological hurdle.

CHAPTER EIGHT

A DAY MADE
IN HEAVEN

THE FRENCH AND BRITISH GRANDS PRIX

Given the way the season had worked out so far, it should have been no surprise to find the first two weeks in July putting me through all kinds of emotion once more. But, this time, I was to end a fairly difficult period on a tremendous high when I won the British Grand Prix at Silverstone for the first time. My father had never done it in seventeen attempts. I felt I had settled the score for the Old Man and filled an important hole in the family CV. Sunday, 10 July 1994 was to be one of the greatest days of my life.

It was almost a month since the Canadian Grand Prix and, during that period, we had the unusual luxury of a three-week break between Montreal and the seventh round of the championship in France. Of course, in typical Formula One style, everyone had been working flat out, with a three-day test session at Silverstone being the focal point.

If Nigel was being offered as a means of comparison, then I would make that work in my favour

Shortly after the test, I visited the Williams factory – and bumped into Nigel Mansell. He had just flown in from the United States and it was no surprise to find him there since I had been told that Nigel would be joining the team for the French Grand Prix. The way Frank explained it to me was that there was pressure from Renault to have Nigel on board for their home race. Renault wanted to make the most of the interest Nigel would undoubtedly generate. But, underlying that, there was, I believe, the belief that Nigel would jump into the car and show me how to do it. I think they thought he would simply go out and win the race.

Initially, I viewed this as a kick in the crotch. I felt very strongly that, under the circumstances, I had been doing as good a job as could be expected and I didn't need to have someone like Nigel come along and show me how to do it. Nevertheless, I understood the commercial reasoning behind the decision. There was a huge amount of hype surrounding Nigel's return to Formula One after eighteen months spent racing Indycars. Several thousand people turned up in the middle of the week to watch him test the Williams at Brands Hatch; a truly incredible endorsement of his pulling power.

The focus was definitely on Nigel and that allowed me simply to get on with my job. Nigel's comeback was generating a great deal of interest in Formula One but it

quickly became apparent that this would also provide me with the perfect opportunity in which to show myself in a good light. If Nigel was being offered as a means of comparison, then I would make that work in my favour. I knew how I had shown against Ayrton Senna and I knew how I had compared with Alain Prost. I was also aware that Alain and Nigel had been quite evenly matched during their time at Ferrari so, all in all, that gave me a great deal of encouragement.

Of course, Nigel had to get over the handicap of having very little experience with the latest Williams but, even so, that did not seem to stand in his way. The first day of practice at Magny-Cours proved difficult for Nigel as he got to grips with the car. As far as I was concerned, the most important aspect was the fact that Nigel was complaining - quite forcefully - about the car's weak points and, in doing so, confirming everything I had been saying all along.

Nigel made one or two useful suggestions drawn from ten years of Formula One experience, but he was not putting his finger on anything new. However, he was able

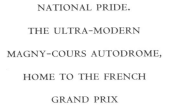

NATIONAL PRIDE.
THE ULTRA-MODERN
MAGNY-COURS AUTODROME,
HOME TO THE FRENCH
GRAND PRIX

A DAY MADE IN HEAVEN

to reach his conclusions very quickly and he was positive and definite about what he wanted. It was impressive to watch Nigel put all that knowledge into action at a race meeting. And it was a relief for me and the team to have someone else highlight the direction we should be going with the car. Of course, we still had the problem of how actually to achieve the improvements in handling we all agreed were necessary.

LIFE IN THE OLD DOG YET

I had been about one second a lap quicker than Nigel on the first day and he was probably smarting from that. But he is irrepressible and, once again, he could put all of his experience to good use. I knew he would go away, think about it overnight and come back much stronger the following day. That was exactly what happened. Saturday was much tougher. And very dramatic.

The second day of practice was cooler, which meant the faster track conditions would make Friday's times irrelevant. Nigel was quicker than me during the morning practice session but I was not unduly concerned since I knew he was running with less fuel on board. I felt good about the car; the changes we had made were positive and

I was looking forward to a tremendous battle during final qualifying in the afternoon.

It all went wrong as soon as I left the pits. Accelerating down the back straight for the first time, I went to change from fifth gear to sixth – and discovered that two fifth gears had been fitted. I returned immediately to the pits, knowing that the error would take some time to rectify. Changing the gear ratios is not the work of a moment because the rear suspension is fixed to the gearbox casing and it is necessary to more or less open up the back end of the car. I knew it could be done faster than you might imagine but, even so, the qualifying session lasted for just one hour and I had already lost several minutes discovering the problem in the first place. What I did not know was that

GEARBOX PROBLEMS
IN QUALIFYING CAUSE ME TO
OVERHEAT

A   DAY   MADE   IN   HEAVEN

FRENCH COOKING.
FRANCE WAS THE HOTTEST RACE
OF THE YEAR, MAKING WATER A
HIGHLY APPRECIATED COMMODITY

the act of finding another fifth gear instead of sixth had actually over-revved the engine. They didn't tell me that at the time, which, perhaps, was just as well since my heart would have sunk completely, knowing the edge might have been taken off the engine's performance.

As it was, I had to stand around and watch the competition go faster and faster, Nigel in particular doing a very impressive job as he claimed pole position. I decided to get out of everyone's way in the garage and get my head into gear by watching from the pit wall. I hadn't been there very long when Jos Verstappen tried to join us by coming over the wall in his Benetton.

Verstappen had lost control coming out of the last corner and he crashed into the wall in front of the Williams pit. It gave me a massive fright and, as I ducked down, I could see a front wheel fly up from the Benetton and hit the back of the television monitors used by the McLaren team in the pit alongside. There were bits flying in all directions and people leaping off the pit wall, all of which had my adrenalin on full surge – not that I needed any assistance in that department.

When I finally got into the car with twenty minutes remaining, I was confident that my first lap would be good enough for pole. That turned out to be the case but then Nigel beat my time by three-tenths of a second on his last run. I knew it was going to be extremely difficult to go even quicker. I threw everything into my final lap – plenty of 'wellie' everywhere, sliding over the kerbs – and, when I came to the final corner, I could feel it was going to be very close.

The last corner is a very slow right-hander and the finishing line is just beyond it. Normally, you would make a clean exit in order to be quick on to the straight which follows. But, in this case, it

Nigel was one of the first to congratulate me but he also knew that he had done an excellent job

was simply a matter of hurling the car out of the corner and breaking the timing beam as soon as possible. It didn't matter that the method might be untidy and unorthodox; it was rather like a runner lunging across the finishing line. I floored the throttle and the car almost flew over the kerb. It looked very spectacular and earned a lot of appreciation because everyone likes to see a car being abused. But it was also very effective; I had won my first pole position of the season in difficult circumstances and against tough opposition. It was a very satisfying moment.

Nigel was very relaxed and upbeat about the whole thing. He was one of the first to congratulate me but he also knew that he had done an excellent job by coming back after so long and extracting that sort of performance from a Formula One car. That was important to him and winning pole was important to me. Renault were delighted because their cars were on the front row at home. Everyone was happy!

Nigel had also removed doubts about the effect of his presence on my championship battle with Schumacher. The last thing I wanted was to have Mansell take away points from me but he went on record as saying he would not hesitate to help me win the race. It was a magnanimous gesture to make in public. Apart from giving me an added boost, it brought the realization that the weekend could be even better than I had imagined. Not only was there the chance that I could win the race, but also Nigel was in a position to take even more points away from Michael by finishing second. That plan was to be blown apart from the very moment the starting lights flicked to green.

I thought I had made a really good start but Schumacher made the most astonishing getaway from the second row. He blasted between Nigel and me and arrived at the first corner in the lead. Heaven knows how he managed to get off the line as quickly as that. It was the kind of start that made a big impression on many seasoned observers as it was so good and provoked comments such as those made by my displaced team-mate, David Coulthard, who was commentating on the event for Eurosport. When asked by the regular commentators John Watson and Allard Kalff what he

SPECTACULAR CONFUSION PUTS ALESI AND BARRICHELLO OUT OF THE RACE

thought of Michael's start, David said that it reminded him of the kind of starts we had been used to seeing the year before, before traction control was outlawed. Whatever the reason, we were back to square one and chasing after the Benetton once more. I had wanted to finish ahead of Nigel, of course, and when he began to drop back because of problems with his car, that effectively ruled him out of the equation. But beating Nigel would be no consolation if, ultimately, I finished behind Schumacher.

We ran a very fast opening phase as I hung on to Michael's coat tails. I could see him missing an apex occasionally at some of the corners and locking his brakes from time to time. It was clear he was pushing as hard as he could and I knew we were at the point where, if he made an error, I could slip through and take the lead. We were really putting Benetton under pressure.

Then came the time for my first pit stop and, by coincidence, Michael came in at the end of exactly the same lap. His stop was fractionally faster than mine and that was to be the beginning of the end as far as the Williams challenge for the lead was concerned. My car started to understeer slightly on the second set of tyres and the Benetton

began to pull away. I held on as best I could but it was obvious that, barring some misfortune for Benetton, I would have to settle for second place.

At the time, it seemed that yet another victory had virtually sealed the championship in Schumacher's favour. We needed to win in France in order to have any hope of turning the tide but Michael's sixth win in seven starts had made his position even stronger. Nevertheless, I had shown myself in a respectable light in the face of a challenge from Mansell and I had at least been able to challenge Schumacher for part of the race. I felt I had impressed the people who needed to be impressed. It had added weight to my credibility in Formula One.

And yet, despite all this, there was a persistent feeling among observers not familiar with Formula One that Nigel had turned the team around and he alone had been responsible for Williams achieving a respectable result. With no disrespect to Nigel, that simply was not true. He had indeed done a very good job on a personal level but the reason we had been competitive in France was because the team had worked damned hard to find a way forward. A number of things had come together, not least

ZANARDI ESCAPES FROM HIS FUMING LOTUS AFTER HAVING DRIVEN FOR HALF A LAP WITH THE CAR ON FIRE. THE MARSHAL IS NOT CLAPPING

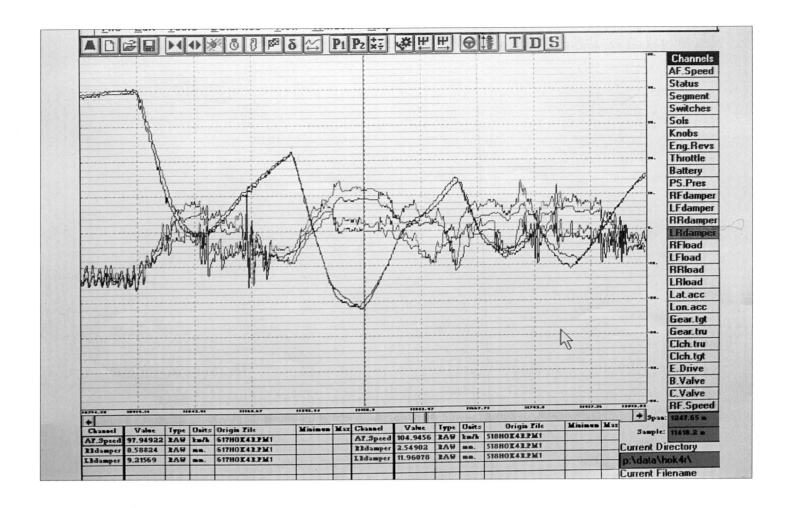

The following text appears within the software interface image:

Channels
AF.Speed
Status
Segment
Switches
Sols
Knobs
Eng.Revs
Throttle
Battery
PS.Pres
RFdamper
LFdamper
RRdamper
LRdamper
RFload
LFload
RRload
LRload
Lat.acc
Lon.acc
Gear.tgt
Gear.tru
Clch.tru
Clch.tgt
E.Drive
B.Valve
C.Valve
RF.Speed

Span: 1247.65 m
Sample: 11418.2 m
Current Directory
p:\data\hok4r\
Current Filename

Channel	Value	Type	Units	Origin File	Minimum	Max	Channel	Value	Type	Units	Origin File	Minimum	Max
AF.Speed	97.94922	RAW	km/h	617HOK4RPM1			AF.Speed	104.9456	RAW	km/h	518HOK4RPM1		
RRdamper	0.58824	RAW	mm.	617HOK4RPM1			RRdamper	2.54902	RAW	mm.	518HOK4RPM1		
LRdamper	9.21569	RAW	mm.	617HOK4RPM1			LRdamper	11.96078	RAW	mm.	518HOK4RPM1		

SEARCHING FOR SPEED.
THIS GRAPH GIVES A COMPARISON
BETWEEN TWO DIFFERENT SET-UPS
ON THE CAR. THE SWOOPING
PEAKS REPRESENT THE CAR'S
SPEED WHILE THE COLOURED
LINES SHOW SUSPENSION
DISPLACEMENTS. UTILIZING THIS
KNOWLEDGE IS NOT AS
STRAIGHTFORWARD AS IT SEEMS

the production of special Renault engines for qualifying. Our performance at Magny-Cours had been the result of much sweat on both sides of the English Channel.

It is true that Nigel's presence had given me an added incentive, but that did not get away from the fact that my motivation was driven by the desire to beat Schumacher. I didn't need the carrot and stick routine; the carrot was quite enough. It irked me, therefore, to discover that the truth of the matter had not been recognized by the majority of the sports commentators. Added to this, there was speculation about Nigel's return to Formula One in 1995 and the question of who would lose out in the job stakes between Hill and Coulthard. I had a lot of respect for David's ability but I felt I was better qualified. It was pretty insulting to find that the question had arisen in the first place, never mind having it suggested that I would be the loser when it came to finding a partner for Mansell, should he return in 1995.

All of this came on top of a struggle to impress upon Frank Williams and Patrick

Head that, if they would commit themselves to backing me, I could fulfil the role of Number One driver. This had arisen following the loss of Ayrton on 1 May. Even though I didn't particularly welcome the added responsibility – the job in just my second full season being difficult enough as it was – I could see that my career had been forced through circumstances to a point where I had to grasp the nettle. I was more than willing to do that even though the chances of beating Schumacher were not being helped by dealing with a car which was taking time to work into a fully competitive state. And yet it seemed to me that everything I did was being regarded with suspicion. It was as if I hadn't

Some of the press thought I had gone through some kind of Jekyll and Hyde transformation

really impressed people enough. I found that unjust; hurtful, even. With the British Grand Prix only a matter of days away, I needed enthusiastic support, not a lot of nasty sniping. So I marched into Silverstone determined to sort this out once and for all.

An informal briefing with the press had become a regular feature on the day before practice began and I used the occasion at Silverstone to forcefully push my message across. I think the journalists were quite shocked. Certainly, they didn't expect anything like this and some of them thought I had gone through some kind of Jekyll and Hyde transformation. In actual fact, the fiery side is in there all the time; it's simply that I don't expose it. I'm not the bolshy sort. I try to be as nice as I can as often as circumstances permit. I don't suffer fools gladly but, at the same time, my approach has always been to smile and say, 'Yes, I hear what you are saying, but now look at what I've done in the car. Look at the results. *This* is what it's all about.'

This plainly had not worked in the past. Hype – the bullshit factor, if you like – often counts for much more than it should do. I had adapted my tactics to suit, even though I don't like employing such methods simply to gain the recognition I feel I deserve. The result was back page news on Friday morning with one or two sensational tabloid headlines such as 'Damon's Gone Nuts!' It was very amusing but, clearly, the serious point had been made. It was, in its way, valuable PR on the eve of the most important race of the season.

One or two people felt that I had created a rod for my own back. Having forcefully stated my case, I now had to deliver and that would produce additional pressure during a weekend which is difficult enough for British drivers. I didn't see it that way. In fact, I felt so much better having got everything off my chest. It had been bottled up inside and I had actually shed a lot of pressure by making my feelings known. As I

PROUD TO BE BRITISH.
CAMPING IS AN ESSENTIAL PART
OF SILVERSTONE. (NOT THE BEST
PART, SOME MIGHT SAY)

climbed into the car for the first practice session, I felt in an attacking mood. This was the moment everyone had been waiting for; the start of the British Grand Prix weekend. I left the pits, got to the first corner – and the front suspension fell apart!

I was going slowly during what we call the installation lap, which is simply a matter of doing one lap and returning to the pits to check for leaks and generally ensuring that everything on the car is in order. I didn't get that far because there had been an assembly problem with the front suspension. The upper part of the suspension, which resists the turning effect created when the brakes are applied, was not attached properly to either side of the car. As soon as I touched the brakes, the front suspension turned and then pulled away from the chassis. As a result, the car started bouncing around with the offending pieces of suspension twanging about in the air. It was impossible to get the car back to the pits without endangering other drivers as they came by at 150 mph, so I had no option but to lurch to the side of the track.

At first I was thinking: 'What have I done? What have I done?' I simply could not

BACK ON TWO WHEELS.
THE ONLY WAY TO GET AROUND
THE PADDOCK QUICKLY

work out what had gone wrong. I got a lift back to the pits in a van and just as we were passing the car park I saw Patrick Head, briefcase and papers in hand, on his way to the pits, just like some commuter walking out of Waterloo station. I said to the driver, 'Let me out here – this is the bloke I want to see!'

Patrick couldn't understand what was happening. The session had only just begun and here I was, helmet in hand, at the back of the paddock. His first thought must have been that I had spun off and he found it equally hard to take on board my explanation of the problem. It soon became obvious that human error was to blame.

There was no point in ranting and raving; the person concerned was absolutely mortified. I have a great deal of respect and affection for mechanics, largely because I have spent much of my life associated with them, either through my father's career as a driver and entrant, or as a competitor myself. These guys do all the hard work, all the graft, but they receive very little acclaim for their efforts. And that's quite apart from the fundamental fact that the driver is putting his life in their hands.

A car can be designed within the limits which make it perfectly safe but if someone forgets to tighten a nut, then the driver has a potential problem. That sort of thing is always at the back of a mechanic's mind. You can see it as he constantly checks and double checks and refuses to allow the car on to the track until he is one hundred per cent certain the job has been done correctly. But nobody is infallible and, from time to time, things can be forgotten or overlooked. When that happens, it knocks a massive hole in a mechanic's pride in his work. Drivers have to accept that they are not operating in a perfect world.

Naturally, you don't want anything to go wrong on the car and you have every right to get very angry and upset when it happens. But, at the same time, you have to remember that it has not been done on purpose, just as a driver does not deliberately make an error when at the wheel. The difference, however, is that the driver is putting his own neck on the line.

The relationship between a driver and his mechanics is usually jovial but at the same time quite often strained because the driver is the person giving them the hard work. And yet, if I want the car changed from back to front, and I want it done before qualifying, they won't question it. The job will be done. The boys working on my car call themselves 'The Floyds' for reasons which I have never clearly understood! They have always been The Floyds and, when I won my first race, I became a Floyd too. It is a sort of private joke among these four and it sums up the friendly but strong rivalry within a team as the mechanics working on the various cars compete with each other. There is a lot of pride at stake but, nevertheless, they enjoy any success which comes the way of the sister car.

The mechanics give you a great deal of encouragement and, if the going gets tough, then the guys working on my car offer one hundred per cent moral support. It's unwavering and something which cannot be bought. You know that every time you climb into the car, they want you to give it stick and get the best result for them and for yourself. They want to be able to wave two fingers at everybody else and prove what a good job they are doing. Without being over-friendly, it's a very close relationship; a tight little team within a team.

Mechanics work under huge pressure and things have to be right first time. If you come into the pits fifteen minutes before the end of practice and ask for a change of

The boys working on my car call themselves 'The Floyds' for reasons which I have never clearly understood!

springs, you know you will need five minutes at the end to actually spend time on the track. So they have to set to work straight away on a car which is very hot. They are aware that they will get burned fingers but they know exactly how to get the springs off and replace them in double-quick time, put everything back together correctly and not forget anything. It's not romantic. Despite being at the sharp end of a high-profile business, mechanics are not starry-eyed by any means. They will bring you down to earth if you get up on your high horse. They will remind you that you haven't bought them a drink lately. . .

There was no banter, however, on that first morning at Silverstone. What made it worse was the fact that we had to hang around until the car could be retrieved during the fifteen-minute break halfway through the session. Then much of the remainder of morning practice was spent fixing the car and I had only four laps right at the end in which to get a feel of the car and prepare myself for the first qualifying session. Even so, I was fourth quickest and, in a way, that helped because I had to attack the circuit and throw

NO ROOM TO WORK; NO TIME TO LOSE. THE WILLIAMS MECHANICS WORK QUICKLY AND EFFICIENTLY WITHIN THE HOT AND RESTRICTED QUARTERS AT THE BACK OF THE CAR the car around. It was terrific fun doing that and I was a little bit wild in places but at least I had managed some running after just about the worst start you could imagine.

I finished the opening qualifying session in fourth place behind Schumacher's Benetton and the Ferraris of Gerhard Berger and Jean Alesi. It might not have been the sort of dominating performance which everyone, particularly the press, would have expected but, under the circumstances, I knew I had done a good job. More than that, I was happy about my driving and I felt very confident.

Part of motor racing is the bitter disappointment which comes all too frequently. But that's what makes the victories so sweet

On Saturday, I worked very hard with Patrick Head and my engineer, John Russell, to try to improve the car and it was one of those rewarding occasions when everything we did seemed to go in the right direction. Come final practice, I genuinely felt we had a chance of taking pole position. If I thought final qualifying seven days before in France had been exciting, then this was to be something else again.

I had allowed myself three runs of two laps each. I left the last run until about ten minutes to go and, by then, Berger was on pole with an astonishing time of 1m 24.980s. If you consider that we had been lapping in the 1m 27s region during the test session, the two-second difference highlights how you extend yourself a lot more than you realize during qualifying. I had got to within three-tenths of Gerhard's time during my first run so I shut my visor and thought: 'This is it.' There was no way I wanted to feel at the end of this final lap that I could have gone fractionally faster at some point, so I simply hurled the car around the place and gave it everything I possibly could. I beat his time by two-hundredths of a second!

I knew, however, that both Michael and Gerhard each had one run left so I was far from celebrating even though my lap had been a good one. I had a bit of luck when Berger managed to damage his Ferrari and puncture a tyre while leaving the pit lane, so that literally knocked him out of the equation. But Schumacher was on the track, putting the Benetton on its metaphorical door-handles.

He came to within three-thousandths of a second of beating my time on his first lap. And he still had one lap remaining. My heart was in my mouth. I was terrified that he would find that fraction of a second but, by the same token, I knew that his tyres had been at their very best only during that first lap. By the halfway mark he was two-tenths faster. I could hardly bear to watch the television monitor. Then, on the very last section of the circuit, he lost a bit of time. I was on pole position for the British Grand Prix.

I was simply ecstatic. There was the thought that, even if things didn't work out well during the race, at least I had won pole position at Silverstone. And yet, somehow, I knew I was being presented with a wonderful opportunity. Part of motor racing is the bitter disappointment which comes all too frequently. But that's what makes the victories so sweet and I just felt, throughout the weekend, that everything was coming together at precisely the right moment. I got out of bed on Sunday morning and I simply had this gut feeling that I was going to win this race.

I wasn't quickest during the warm-up but that did not seem to matter. The car was working extremely well and I didn't feel the need to push hard. Our primary concern was race tactics and we gave very serious thought to a suitable tactical plan. Naturally, we could remember all too clearly how Schumacher had beaten us off the line in France. So, assuming he repeated such an incredible feat, the question was how to win the race from second place? It was decided that we should attack as hard as possible in the opening part of the race, which meant starting with a light load of fuel and making an early first pit stop. We were ready to take on all comers. I was going to make the very best of this wonderful opportunity.

Other people seemed to realize that too. Derek Warwick came up to me on the grid and wished me luck. Racing drivers are very selfish people and sometimes when they pass on good wishes, you are aware of a twinge of insincerity. But Derek is a nice guy and I knew that he was being completely genuine. He had led the British Grand Prix briefly while racing with Toleman in 1982 but he had never won a Grand Prix. I knew he would dearly love to have had a chance such as mine and Derek was the first to recognize that you have to make the best use of whatever luck comes your way. That's why I was determined not to squander this unique situation because I owed it not only to myself and everyone in the team, but also to people like Derek who have never had the same opportunity. I really meant it when I said during an interview on the grid that it was a lovely day to win the British Grand Prix. That wonderful feeling of inner confidence was growing stronger and stronger.

Certainly, I didn't feel I needed assistance of any kind. I was most surprised, therefore, when Schumacher shot past me as we set off on the warm-up lap. The rules say that drivers cannot overtake although sometimes that can't be helped if the man in front of you is slow to get away, in which case you drop back into position as soon as possible. But this was blatant. He rushed ahead, with me giving chase, the pair of us running almost flat out for half a lap. Then he slowed down after going through Stowe corner and I resumed my position – only to have Michael blast past me again just after we had come out of Club corner.

When we lined up on the grid, the start was delayed because David Coulthard had stalled. That sort of thing is a dreadful anti-climax because, as you might imagine, your adrenalin is at peak level just before the start. Suffering a delay is like deflating a hot-air balloon; you sag a little and then spend the next five minutes pumping yourself up again while waiting for the re-start.

We went through the formalities once more – and Michael did exactly the same thing. I couldn't believe it. I had told the team about his earlier misdemeanours and I got on the radio once more and said that he had quite blatantly overtaken me yet again. I thought nothing more about the matter because it was no longer my business. My job was to get off the line faster than anyone else and go on to win this race.

I fully expected a repeat performance of Schumacher's starts in most of the previous races as he streaked off the line without a hint of wheelspin and took the inside line (my pole position was on the left) for the first right-hander. If he managed that, then he would be hard to beat. My start worked very well but, as I headed towards the first corner I kept looking in my mirror, and then across to my right, wondering where Michael had got to. As I turned into the corner it became clear he had not made a good start. This weekend just seemed to get better and better.

The intention now was to really hammer the first fifteen laps. But Schumacher obviously had the same plan and he was right behind me. I was quicker than him on some parts of the track, he was faster in one section in particular. Overall, we were well matched but I felt I had the measure of the Benetton.

We lost our tactical advantage during the first pit stop when the Benetton got in and out of the pits faster than we could manage. Fortunately, though, Michael got caught behind Gerhard Berger, who was now leading but planned to make his first stop later than ours. As a result, Schumacher was held up and I was able to close the gap. That bit of luck aside, there was nothing to chose between Michael and me in lap times.

Then the cards fell his way slightly when I was held up very badly by back-markers. He was about three seconds ahead of me – and now leading the race because Berger had made his pit stop – when I saw the black flag being displayed with Schumacher's number. There is no ambiguity over this signal; it means: 'Stop at the end of the next lap'. To my great surprise, Michael carried on. When he failed to come in after three or four laps, I thought: 'He's playing with fire here.' Nonetheless, I was not going to make any assumptions and I pressed on, determined not to let him get away. I was still with Schumacher when he disappeared into the pits for a five-second stop-go penalty in connection with his antics on the formation lap.

Once again, I couldn't believe my luck. It was clear that my chances of winning were stronger than ever and I did not want to let Schumacher reduce the 20-second lead which I now held. And yet I wanted to look after this race as if I was holding a baby. I was taking great care with everything I did while, at the same time, pushing hard to maintain the gap over the Benetton. At one point, the gap came down to 15.4 seconds but I was able to slug it out with him and stretch the lead back to 17.7 seconds. When it stayed that way with seven or eight laps to go, I knew it would be safe enough to back off slightly.

As I came towards the end of my final lap, the counter on the dashboard said I had one lap to go. My pit board said I had two laps remaining. I asked for clarification on the radio and the team said they would check. As I approached the finishing line I could see an official standing with the flag. But it was furled. So I decided to press

on. Then, just as I went by, he suddenly unfurled the flag and waved it. That meant I missed the opportunity of crossing the line with my arms in the air and generally going berserk. I was back on the radio asking if there was another lap. 'No,' they said. 'That's it. You've won the British Grand Prix!' It was the most incredible feeling to hear those words.

THANKING THE MEN WHO ASK
ONLY ONE THING OF YOU:
TO TAKE THEIR CAR ACROSS
THE LINE FIRST

The reception from the crowd was magnificent. Halfway round the slowing down lap, a marshal stepped forward to hand me a massive Union Jack attached to what looked like a twelve-foot length of 4"x2"! The rules say that you are not supposed to stop en route to parc ferme at the finish so I just managed to keep the car rolling while I collected this red, white and blue bed-sheet! A Formula One car can do 100 mph in first gear so it didn't take too much effort to create a lot of drag from this flag. Having

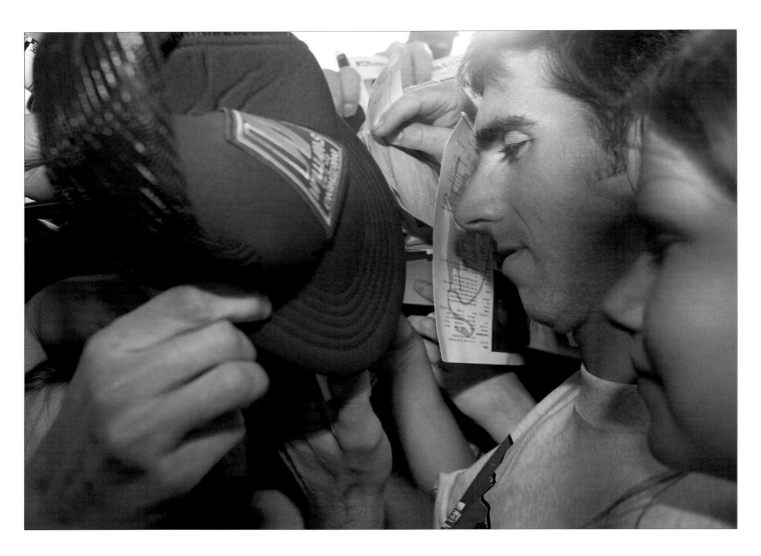

SIGN YOUR WAY OUT OF THIS

ONE, HILL

just completed a Grand Prix, I was quite tired; it was impossible to hold the thing up, steer the car and wave at the same time! But I managed somehow and reached parc ferme for the start of celebrations which lasted long into the evening.

Georgie was there to give me a big hug and a kiss. Then it was up to the podium to receive the trophy from Princess Diana and, once Her Royal Highness had been escorted to a safe distance, it was on with the happy ritual of champagne spraying. It was, without question, the best moment of my life. On top of this I had received a trophy which my father would have loved to have won – and my mother and two sisters were there to see me do it.

The entire weekend had been one hundred per cent positive and I had suddenly struck a rich vein of confidence – and enjoyment, too – which had been missing for

THE BRITISH GRAND PRIX

quite a while. I signed autographs non-stop and really let myself go. Later that evening, I was bass guitar in Eddie Jordan's brother-in-law's band, playing good old-fashioned rock and roll on a stage adapted from a lorry trailer in the paddock (they had obviously been on the road!). Johnny Herbert and Eddie Irvine were on the stage too, as was my sister Brigitte who was gyrating wildly, and Eddie Jordan was on drums.

So in one day I fulfilled two lifetime ambitions: winning the British Grand Prix and playing in a band to an appreciative audience of more than ten people. I think I brought something quite unique to the musical entertainment on that beautiful English summer evening. It had been a special day. The evening was warm and still and the sun was just going down in a clear sky. It was as close to perfection as you would wish. For me, it was the end of a day made in heaven.

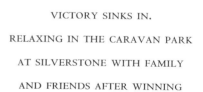

VICTORY SINKS IN.
RELAXING IN THE CARAVAN PARK
AT SILVERSTONE WITH FAMILY
AND FRIENDS AFTER WINNING

A DAY MADE IN HEAVEN

CHAPTER NINE

FITNESS AND FIRES

THE GERMAN AND HUNGARIAN GRANDS PRIX

By good fortune, there was a three-week break between Silverstone and the German Grand Prix. Usually it is a case of getting straight back to work and concentrating on the next race in a fortnight's time but, on this occasion, the long gap by Formula One standards allowed plenty of time to enjoy my victory.

Apart from spending the first few days walking on a cloud, completely impervious to anything that might trouble me, I did put the time to good use. We moved out of Wandsworth to a much larger house in Ascot. They say that moving house is very stressful but this was the ideal time to do it and the memories of the British Grand Prix victory seemed to ease many of the potential worries. The weather was perfect and we spent quite a lot of time together as a family; the whole thing slotted very nicely into the gap between the races.

However, I did have some important business to attend to when I was called to Paris to answer questions about picking up the Union Flag during my slowing down lap at Silverstone. That may sound an innocuous offence but the aim of the rule – which says the car must not stop on its way to parc ferme – is to prevent a driver from taking on board some foreign body which might increase the weight of the car. The cars must weigh no less than 505 kgs at any time, the aim being to stop unscrupulous designers from sacrificing weight for speed. Obviously, the lighter the car is, the faster it will go and, without a minimum weight limit, the temptation might prove too much.

So, the rule has some justification although I knew that, while I had gone very slowly, I had not come to a standstill. We had evidence from the marshal who had to run alongside in order to give me the flag. And we also had the footage from the onboard camera which showed quite clearly that the wheels did not stop revolving. My case was

Barrichello and Hakkinen had apparently left Silverstone without first reporting to the Stewards, an offence I was not actually aware of myself

therefore pretty solid. In fact, I tried to get out of going to Paris because I had done nothing wrong and it was a day gone from my schedule but, in the event, I had to attend and it turned out to be an interesting experience.

There was quite a gathering. Four of us had been hauled up before this meeting of the FIA World Council. Michael Schumacher was there to answer the serious charge of ignoring the black flag at Silverstone, while Rubens Barrichello and Mika Hakkinen, involved in a collision on the last lap of the British Grand Prix, had apparently left the circuit without first reporting to the Stewards, an offence I was not actually aware of myself, and presumably neither were they!

I had never been to the FIA headquarters in the Place de la Concorde before and, at first glance, it is an impressive sight, situated in a governmental area similar in some ways to Westminster. As you enter, there is historical reference all around to races and champions of the past; all very grand and imposing. But, as soon as you go upstairs, the steps creak and the wallpaper is fading. You have to wait in a tatty old room which is reminiscent of the civil service rather than the governing body of world motor sport. The room was packed, Benetton winning hands down by bringing along most of their designers, team managers, the driver and the team principal; everyone, it seemed, but the mechanics.

I must admit to having a slight air of invincibility because I knew I had not broken any rules – and I could prove it. But, even so, the business of having to sit and wait with Ian Harrison, our team manager, and the team's barrister, reminded me of being hauled up before the headmaster. The waiting was part of the torture. I saw Hakkinen and Barrichello emerge, each with a suspended-one-race ban, and I began to wonder if I was right in believing I had nothing to fear. The feeling of trepidation accelerated when I took my turn and walked into the room.

There were about twenty-five people – various heads of motor sporting bodies worldwide who could make the trip – sitting around a massive table. Opposite me sat Max Mosley, the President of the FIA. To my left was Bernie Ecclestone, the FIA's Vice-President of Promotional Affairs, and beside him, Jean Todt, Ferrari's sporting director. I never did get to the bottom of why he was there. To Todt's left sat Jean-Marie Balestre, a former president of the FIA, and so on, round the table. Everyone had headsets so that the proceedings could be translated into various languages. There was a video screen in the corner. As I took my seat, I thought: 'Jeez, this is serious!'

My brief then went into his defence while Bernie Ecclestone kept whispering, 'Tell him to shut up!'

Max opened the proceedings by saying he did not believe I had done anything seriously wrong because I did not actually stop the car. That left me wondering what I could possibly say to defend myself because the judge had virtually admitted that I had been called to Paris for no reason! My brief then went into his defence while Bernie Ecclestone kept whispering, 'Tell him to shut up!' It really was quite extraordinary. Someone said they would like to see a video of the incident and, after that had been shown, Max said, 'Thank you very much. Have you got anything to say?'

I took a deep breath and said that I understood why the rule was necessary. But I asked everyone present to bear in mind that this had been my home Grand Prix and it was a very proud moment for me. I said I thought every driver in such circumstances should at least have the right to carry their national flag – at which point, I got a 'Hear, Hear!' – I think – from Jean-Marie Balestre! Once I had finished my little speech, I was asked to wait outside. On my return, Max Mosley said, 'You did not actually break the rules, so there is nothing we can do. But we think that you went against the spirit of the regulations. However, nothing will be done. Goodbye.'

Of course, they had left Michael Schumacher until last. On my way out, I told him I would not gain satisfaction from any benefit which would come to me from a race ban or whatever they decided to impose on him. I said I wanted him to know that, wished him luck, and then left. I didn't hang around until Michael's case had been heard because I did not want to appear to be gloating over what, it seemed to me, was going to an inevitable punishment of some sort.

Nevertheless, because of the outcome of my own hearing, I walked out of the building with a smile on my face. The man from the *Sun* was there, complete with a couple of Page 3 girls and a Union Jack for me to wave. It was a light-hearted affair and, with the British Grand Prix victory still fresh in my mind, I enjoyed the moment.

By all accounts, the same could not be said for Michael when he later emerged into the Place de la Concorde. His six points, earned by finishing second at Silverstone, had been wiped out and he had been given a two-race ban. What made it

For some reason, I was seen by certain people as being to blame for Michael's plight

even worse was the fact that the next race was scheduled for Germany, his home Grand Prix. I sympathized because the race at Hockenheim would mean as much to him as the British Grand Prix had meant to me. It was an important race for Schumacher, as well as the Grand Prix organizers, and here he was, caught between a rock and a hard place.

Benetton had been told that if they appealed against the ban, Schumacher could race in Germany, pending the outcome of the hearing at the end of August. But that brought with it the risk – as had been demonstrated in Eddie Irvine's case following his involvement in the four-car pile-up in Brazil – of an increased sentence if the appeal was rejected. In any case, Irvine's original one-race ban had been for causing an accident and Schumacher's crime in ignoring the black flag – the equivalent of a motorist failing to stop when instructed to do so by the police – had been just as serious. I wasn't surprised by the verdict. In the end, the team appealed and, by the time everyone turned up in Germany for the ninth round of the championship, I had forgotten all about the affair. But feelings continued to run high elsewhere.

For some reason, I was seen by certain people as being to blame for Michael's plight. When I arrived at the circuit for the first time in my Renault Espace, I tried to slip in through the back gate without being recognized, a pretty futile move, as it turned out. At first they shook the car and then banged on the roof with their fists but it soon became good-natured. The Renault was surrounded and they tried to climb in through the back door. Rather foolishly, I had not locked the tailgate and it suddenly occurred to me that my luggage, briefcase, money – everything – was right there and I had no

IT'S A FAIR COP: ONE OF THE
GERMAN POLICEMEN WHO
ESCORTED ME IN AND OUT OF THE
HOCKENHEIMRING SPOTS HIS
OPPORTUNITY FOR A SIGNATURE

way of stopping them. They could have fleeced me on the spot, dragged me from the car if they had wanted to, but everything was fine. I think that summed up the general feeling; the race fans were rowdy but extremely good-natured.

Of course, there is always an exception. On the Friday morning, I was called into the Williams motorhome to talk to Frank and Ian Harrison. They had received a message from the police that a local newspaper had been contacted by an anonymous caller. This person had said, quite simply, that if I qualified ahead of Michael Schumacher then, on Sunday, I would be shot.

At first, I thought it was laughable. But it became less funny when I considered this was Germany and I recalled Monica Seles being stabbed by a fanatical Steffi Graf supporter. It only took one look at the spectator enclosures to see how much they wanted Michael to win. You assume that 99.9 per cent of the fans are sane. But it only takes one hothead to cause chaos. Suddenly, the whole thing was not funny at all.

The police suggested I had an escort to and from the circuit each day. Starting on Friday evening, a police car pulled up outside the motorhome, I leapt inside and we left by a back road. I changed hotel rooms to avoid being registered in my own name, and a Renault security man stayed outside my door all night. As Georgie had not come

SEEKING SANCTUARY.
APART FROM WHEN I'M ALONE IN
THE CAR, ESCAPING INTO THE
TRUCK IS THE ONLY WAY OF
AVOIDING THE CONTINUAL GLARE
OF ATTENTION

FITNESS AND FIRES

on this trip, I called a close friend in England, a big chap named Sheridan Coakley, and said I could do with some company. He very kindly flew out on Saturday and, afterwards, he sent me a book inscribed 'from the human shield'. I think he felt he was there to stop the bullets!

What made matters ten times worse was the fact that I eventually qualified ahead of Schumacher, although not in the manner we had expected. He was fourth on the grid, I was third, and ahead of us were the Ferraris of Gerhard Berger and Jean Alesi. This was a change in the script, the powerful Ferrari V12 coming into its own on the long straights which dominate Hockenheim. I had predicted that might happen but I didn't expect them to be that quick. And, now that Berger was on pole position, he had also landed the penalty clause of a threat to his life. On Saturday evening we shared the same police car out of the circuit!

This was very useful because I got to know Gerhard a bit better. Although we are colleagues, in a manner of speaking, drivers rarely get the chance to enjoy each

other's company during a race weekend, each driver being completely bound up with the task of beating everyone else. This chauffeur-driven ride home may not have been a jolly social occasion but at least it was the ideal opportunity to have a chat.

I told Gerhard he looked tired and he replied that if I had been driving for Ferrari as long as he had, I would look just as rough. Gerhard is a fairly happy-go-lucky character but not even he was prepared to take any risks when it came to receiving death threats – although I got the impression he actually enjoyed the element of living dangerously.

I found little difficulty in putting the whole thing to the back of my mind while driving the Williams. But I had completely forgotten about the drivers' parade on race morning. The routine is that we leave the official drivers' pre-race briefing and go straight to the pit lane, where we climb aboard an open-topped car and get taken round the track – or, in this case, the stadium section. Hockenheim is banana-shaped, the long curving straights interrupted by three chicanes. At the bottom end is the

GRAPHIC DESCRIPTION.
MAX NIGHTINGALE, ONE OF
THE BOFFINS AT WILLIAMS, USES
A GRAPH TO HELP ME
UNDERSTAND THE CAR'S
BEHAVIOUR IN MORE DETAIL

'THERE COULD BE TROUBLE AHEAD'. THE RACE HAS BARELY STARTED AND ALREADY FOUR CARS ARE OUT. WITHIN THE NEXT FEW SECONDS, ANOTHER FIVE WILL BE ELIMINATED, STARTING WITH HAKKINEN'S MCLAREN (FAR LEFT)

There must have been at least 100,000 people in the stadium, and every one of them seemed to be rooting for Michael Schumacher

stadium, laid out just like a football ground with the cars coming in one corner, going through a twisty bit in the middle, passing the pits and then disappearing out the other side to start the long haul to the top end of the circuit.

There must have been at least 100,000 people in the stadium, and every one of them seemed to be rooting for Michael Schumacher. That's all very well but they have the habit of letting off fire crackers and rockets at the slightest opportunity. It was like 5 November during the parade lap and there I was, waving to the crowd and thinking what a perfect target I would make. The Germans were going completely nuts about Michael. When they saw me, they would start booing. Eventually I had had enough of this intimidation. At one point there was a crowd of shirtless, well-lagered supporters hurling abuse from the fence. I gave them the old two fingers and yelled insults in return. That got them suitably wound up. But at least they didn't shoot me.

The police had taken the view that I was actually safer inside the circuit although, during the parade lap, I did have my doubts. I didn't realize it at the time, but I was affected by the whole thing. I did not sleep particularly well the night before the race and I had a slight headache just before the start. I was quite tense and not in particularly good shape during the final hour or two. But, once I was in the car, my concentration was entirely focused.

My start was not brilliant. Not only did Michael get ahead of me but Ukyo Katayama also came through in his Tyrrell. I was fifth, behind Berger, Alesi, Katayama and Schumacher. I could see in my mirrors all sorts of mayhem at the first corner – in fact,

several cars were eliminated on the spot — and I was congratulating myself on having escaped all of that when Alesi's Ferrari blew up a couple of seconds later. I thought: 'That's handy! One Ferrari down, I'm fourth with Schumacher just ahead of me. All I have to do is stick with him. No problem.'

Then going into the chicane, Michael dived into the rapidly closing gap left open by Ukyo Katayama and it looked to me that Ukyo, unaccustomed to running at the front, was being quite co-operative. He got a bit sideways coming out of the second chicane, whereas I made a clean exit and used the Tyrrell's slipstream to pull right up to Katayama on the run towards the third chicane.

I pulled out and went down the inside of the Tyrrell, under-braking for the corner. But he braked incredibly late and got a nose ahead of me. I thought: 'I'd better get out of here and try and slot in behind him.' But then he came across the front of my car and hit my right-front wheel. The impact bent the steering arm. I knew I was more or less out of the race.

I knew straightaway that I had jeopardized everything by trying to take Katayama when I should have been more patient

I limped back to the pits, trying not to risk breaking the other steering arm. When I reached the Williams pit, I found myself playing a part in every team manager's nightmare: both cars parked in the pit road at the end of the first lap. David Coulthard had been caught in that first-corner accident and I had to wait while they fixed his front wing. My repairs would take a lot longer in any case and, when I rejoined, I was a lap and a half behind with no hope of catching up. But I wanted to press on because you can always learn something from a race, no matter where you are in the running order. Besides, we had a new high-revving engine from Renault and this would be a good endurance test, if nothing else.

There was the thought that I might grab a point or two by taking advantage of other people's troubles and sneaking into the top six. When I was out there, I was lapping two seconds faster than Berger, who eventually won the race. In the end, all I had to show for my weekend's work was eighth place.

But what made me feel really cheesed off was the fact that Schumacher had actually dropped out with engine trouble – the first time that had happened to him in a race all season. I knew straightaway that I had jeopardized everything by trying to take Katayama when I should have been more patient. I could have pointed the finger at Ukyo for what he did but the truth was that, even though I thought Schumacher was getting away, I should have sat behind Katayama and waited. I had no one to blame but myself. Hockenheim is a relatively easy circuit on which to overtake. I would have got past the Tyrrell eventually and, the way things turned out, I certainly would have won that race.

However, the talking point of the day had little to do with either the winner or the championship. During the race, I had come into the stadium and been startled to see a column of black smoke rising above the pits, a sure sign that a car had caught fire during refuelling. It struck me that the Paddock Club was directly above the pits and it seemed quite likely that many of the sponsors and their guests would have been peering over the edge, watching the pit stop.

About fifteen seconds later I passed the front of the pits, by which time all I could see was white dust, which meant the fire had been extinguished. But I knew nothing more than that. I learned afterwards that Jos Verstappen and three or four of the Benetton mechanics had received facial burns when a valve failed to close properly and allowed fuel to spray on to the hot car. By sheer good fortune, no one else had been injured.

They said that refuelling in Formula One would be completely safe, but I'm afraid that didn't wash with me

In the weeks to come, there would be a lot of controversy over the incident but, as far as I was concerned, the fire had merely confirmed what I had feared all along. It's like stepping on to an aeroplane and someone trying to assure you that it won't crash. But you know that it is impossible to have something which is 100 per cent safe. Sooner or later, a plane will crash. To my mind, it was exactly the same when refuelling was introduced to Formula One for the 1994 season; a fire was inevitable at some point in the future.

It could hardly be otherwise in a situation where fuel is being pumped as quickly as possible, under pressure, into a racing car. You only need to look at the various forms of motor racing – Le Mans, Indycars – where they refuel during the races. They have all had fires due to fuel being spilled. At the beginning of the season, they said that refuelling in Formula One would be completely safe, but I'm afraid that didn't wash with me. And here was proof of it.

So I was not surprised to see a fire, but I was horrified by its effects when I watched the video later in the week. What struck me most was the fact that Verstappen did not manage to get out of the car even though, at the beginning of the season, we have to prove that we can evacuate the cockpit in five seconds. He didn't appear to move and you could see that, moments earlier, he had opened his visor and fuel had splashed inside, then caught alight, making it impossible for him to see how to undo his seatbelts.

Fire used to be commonplace in Formula One, particularly in the 1950s when the

SOME PEOPLE HAVE MOOSE
HEADS ON THEIR WALLS; SOME
PREFER GUITARS. THE HARRISON
HILLBILLY COWBOYS' FIRST EVER
GIG. HARDLY MUSIC HISTORY IN
THE MAKING . . .

safety standards we take for granted today were unheard of. It was around that time that George Harrison's interest in motor racing was triggered by the running of the British Grand Prix on the roads around the Aintree horse-racing course. The circuit was a short train ride from George's home in Liverpool and, even though his attention was diverted slightly in the 1960s by his association with an obscure beat combo wryly called The Beatles, he never lost his fascination for the sport.

He turns up at a couple of races each year and, when he came to Hockenheim, we got into discussing cars and his business. We had plenty to talk about because my other love is music and guitars and I was delighted when George invited me to his place in Henley for a bit of a session. This took place in his recording studio, where he keeps the most fantastic collection of guitars which he uses to create the right sound for whatever track he happens to be recording. It is a musician's treasure trove. He can pick up a guitar and say: 'We used this one for one of the tracks on *Revolver*,' or, 'That

'IMPROVING YOUR MIND, I SEE,
MR ENFIELD': FRANK DOBERMAN
GROVELS FOR AN AUTOGRAPH.
IT'S ALL PART OF THE ACT . . .

one is from *A Hard Day's Night.*' It was a unique opportunity to be able to strum these guitars and a most special thing to be with the man himself as we banged out a few tunes. Now I think I could make a decent busker on the Underground if the need arose. It's always nice to have something to fall back on.

At around that time, I also tried my hand at a spot of acting. Drivers get various requests to do bits and pieces and one was from Harry Enfield, asking if I would like to take part in a sketch for his television programme. It was a very funny script and I was glad to accept. I was full of anticipation when I went to Brands Hatch for the filming. The problem was, I suddenly realized I would not only have to learn my lines – of which there were very few – but also Harry's lines, because I needed to know when to say my various pieces. I managed to cope after about three or four takes. It was, as you might imagine, a huge amount of fun but I don't think I'm ready for an Equity card yet.

These diversions took me away completely from motor racing for a couple of

NO PAIN, NO GAIN — TRAINING AT
THE HARBOUR CLUB, LONDON

hours. Even though we race, on average, once a fortnight during the season, time in between is usually spent on business related to my job, be it testing, public relations or simply keeping fit.

People sometimes assume from watching television that, because motor racing is a sedentary profession, it does not require much fitness. This could not be further from the truth. Grand Prix racing is physically exhausting because the driver has to brace his body against the continual vertical and sideways loadings for up to two hours. He is constantly having to hold his body in tension and the heart rate is high for the duration of the race because, not only is he working hard physically, there is the mental stress which comes with having to concentrate totally for such a long period.

It is true to say that the best exercise suitable for motor racing is actually driving the cars. That's why it is valuable for a driver to cover many miles during testing, particularly in the off-season. But, while driving the car is vitally important when it comes to developing the right muscles, all drivers need to have a basic level of fitness which is generally achieved in two different ways.

The first is to attain a high level of aerobic fitness which allows the proficient management of oxygen in the blood. The efficient pumping of blood around the body, particularly to the brain, helps to keep a driver sharp and the heart rate low. The less strain applied to the heart, the better the driver will be able to think and concentrate. This is achieved mainly through running, although you don't just set off blindly with no particular objective. It's quite a science and

The effort required to drive the cars is more than in the past because you are going quicker over a longer period of time

calls for a fair amount of information on the subject. It is also possible to improve aerobic fitness through endurance where you exercise for more than forty minutes with your heart rate at the correct level, probably about 160 beats to the minute. As before, the aim is to improve the strength of the heart and the ability to convert oxygen in the blood.

It is also necessary to concentrate on developing arm muscles, which was more important a few years ago when the downforce acting on the car was much higher than it is now. I felt I had the advantage over Alain Prost in 1993 insofar as I was stronger. I had better upper-body endurance and I found that an advantage, particularly towards the end of the races. I spent a considerable time on exercises aimed at strengthening shoulders, forearms and grip. While I wouldn't claim to be the strongest man ever to have sat in a Formula One car, I think I spend my time efficiently in the gym. I train the right parts of my body in order to get the maximum benefit in the short space of time I have available. That's one of the problems for a driver. To be on really top form a driver should work out five days a week but that is simply not possible because of commitments elsewhere.

Of course, there are other means of keeping in shape – weight lifting, swimming, working on a rowing machine – but none of this is much use if the driver becomes ill. As I mentioned earlier in the book, I made a huge effort before the first race of the season, and then picked up a chest infection which made me feel as weak as a kitten in Brazil.

As any athlete will tell you, the problem is that the fitter you are, the more you work your body to the limit and the closer you go to the edge of your body's ability to resist infection. It is necessary to be careful about training to exactly the right level. For a while, early in the season, I was trying to recover from the virus and I deliberately

FAR PARKING.

IT COSTS NOTHING TO PARK IN

HUNGARY BUT VIEWING IS EXTRA

chose not to train too much in order to build up my body resistance. It was not something I wanted to do because I was concerned about my fitness. You get caught between the two options and it is not an easy choice.

Fitness is a complete package of muscle strength and endurance, plus mental strength and generally feeling good about the fact that you have put in the hours of training and are fitter than ever before. You know you have got more stamina and that allows you to push hard on each and every lap during a Grand Prix.

This has been particularly vital in 1994 because, with the introduction of re-fuelling, the cars have been running with only a third or half of the fuel loads compared to last year. The races have been long sprints in between each pit stop, unlike before when the cars were heavy with a full load of fuel in the early stages of each race. The lap times have been quicker and although the downforce has been reduced by the regulation changes, the effort required to drive the cars is more than in the past because you are going quicker over a longer period of time and the cars are more difficult to drive.

The next Grand Prix, at the Hungaroring, a tight, twisting circuit, would be slow but physically demanding, particularly as the race usually lasts the best part of two hours. Once again, however, the racing took a back seat to various issues, the main one being the question of who was to blame for the Hockenheim fire. Just as we were

about to leave for Hungary, it was revealed that the Benetton team had removed a filter from their refuelling rig and, according to the FIA, this had caused the fuel leak.

Benetton did not deny that they had removed the filter; in fact, they claimed they had been given permission to do so. But they also produced a report which said the refuelling equipment was not safe and, all told, the team defended themselves quite vigorously. The fact still remained that the filter had been taken out and this in itself may have explained why they had been able to make Michael's pit stop a second quicker then expected.

Because of all this drama surrounding the Benetton team, there was talk of even more race bans in the offing which, in turn, increased the speculation that I would be the main beneficiary. Going into Hungary, I was twenty-seven points behind Schumacher but all of this uncertainty reinforced my wishful thinking about the possibility of me becoming World Champion at the end of the year.

Being realistic about it, I did not see myself as having a really good chance of winning the championship: I had thrown away an important opportunity at Hockenheim. Even so, the way things were beginning to pan out was stoking up the controversy and, if nothing else, keeping the championship alive. And, regardless of the odds, I continued to have a mathematical chance of closing the gap. Besides, I took the view that the important thing was to try to win in Hungary. The track suited the

IF YOU WONDERED WHY WE
NEED TO CHANGE TYRES SO
OFTEN DURING A GRAND PRIX,
THEN PART OF THE REASON IS
ILLUSTRATED HERE. THE BLACK
BLOBS ON THE TRACK ARE BITS
OF TYRE RUBBER . . .

Benetton; a good, nimble car powered by the useful (but not as powerful as the Renault) Ford V8 engine on a circuit where ultimate horsepower was not the vital factor. Michael would undoubtedly get the best out of this combination but if we could win on Benetton territory, without any assistance from regulations and black flags, it would be a severe blow to Benetton, quite apart from being a boost for Williams. The thought was, if ever I had to win a race, then it was this one.

Free from death threats and suchlike, I started off quite well. It rained on the first day of practice, which was unexpected insofar as I hadn't brought any wet weather clothing and yet it was chucking it down when I arrived at the track on Friday morning. The one thing to be said about a good car is that it is generally nice to drive in all conditions. Even though the track was soaking wet, I was able to match Michael's times and enjoy myself in the process by flinging the car around and having a good time.

This was very comforting because it indicated that the car was right. After finishing just a couple of tenths of a second slower than Michael in the first qualifying

session (run in the dry, later in the day), I was pretty confident that I would at least be on the front row of the grid, an important consideration on a circuit which ranks second only to Monaco in terms of being impossible to overtake during the race.

We tried to improve the car for Saturday's qualifying session but, on reflection, we failed to find what we were looking for. I had been hoping to make the car more manageable, the problem being that, on this particular track, the Williams bounced in the middle of the corners and lost grip. One minute you had the car nicely balanced and the next, it hit a bump and suddenly the back wanted to kick out, or the front tried to slide away. It was difficult to stay precisely on the racing line and anywhere else that would not have been the problem it was on the Hungaroring.

Because the circuit is hardly used for racing from one Grand Prix to the next, everywhere off the racing line is dusty and very dirty. The sticky tyres pick up this dirt at the first opportunity, so you have to stay resolutely on the narrow racing line. Elsewhere, you could slide wide by a fraction or two and get away with it. But not at

the Hungaroring. The dirty track also means that fresh tyres give their best performance in the first two laps; after that, they begin to pick up the bits of rubber and general debris and your lap times suffer accordingly.

I allowed myself three runs during the final session, but the first two were blighted by slower cars. I had one run remaining when Schumacher recorded an astonishing time, about 1.5 seconds faster than I had managed up to that point. I had serious doubts about being able to match him but I gave an extra push on that last run, came very close to his time during the first two-thirds of the lap but lost out on the final section by four-tenths of a second. The rest, led by my team-mate David Coulthard, were over a second in arrears; it seemed clear this race would be between Michael and me – and I wanted to win it.

We did a lot of thinking that night. Among the permutations which crossed my mind was the thought that, supposing I did get ahead of Schumacher at the first corner, he would have nothing to lose by accidentally, as it were, knocking me off the road while trying to overtake. That sort of thing has happened before between protagonists in the fight for a World Championship, notably Alain and Ayrton at Suzuka in 1990. Although I had no reason to believe that Michael would do such a thing, one has to be prepared for all eventualities.

I had serious doubts about being able to match Michael but I gave an extra push on that last run

But the most important consideration was the question of pit stops. We took the view, as a team, that two refuelling stops would be the answer. Our calculations suggested that, by taking the lap time of the slowest car, and adding 30 seconds or so because that's how far he would be behind the leader at the end of the first lap, I would have caught the backmarkers by about lap 15. Given that one wants to stop as few times as possible and the race is 77 laps, the first stop would need to be at about lap 25 if you plan a two-stop race. However, at a place like Hungary, overtaking even the slowest of cars is difficult and will lose the leader several seconds per lap. A decision about the number of stops is made on the basis of whether the gain in performance from running less fuel (i.e., weight) will be cancelled out by the penalty of having to stop an additional time in the pits, a delay which could be 25 seconds or more, depending on the circuit.

I later wished that I had followed my gut instinct and opted to stop three times

Throughout our deliberations, I had a growing feeling that Michael was going to make three stops because that seemed to be right after considering the traffic factor. Even though my experience in this area was very limited, I later wished that I had followed my gut instinct and opted to stop three times.

However, regardless of refuelling tactics, the most important thing was to try to get into the first corner ahead of the Benetton. If I could do that then, with overtaking severely restricted, Michael would have to stay behind me and that would upset his plans. But it would be easier said than done. By qualifying second, I had to start from the grubby side of the track and, because of the staggered positions on the grid, Schumacher would be a few metres ahead of me on the left – but on the cleaner racing line. To take the lead I would need to get a whole length in front of him so that I could pull over to the left in order to take the best line through the first corner. And, as I explained earlier, I had to make sure I did not provide him with any excuse to bundle me off the road. It was a tall order – but not an impossible one.

My determination to do well was already high when I received an unusual boost to the morale not long before the start of the race. A Brazilian journalist gave me a shirt signed by the captain of Brazil's World Cup football team. The message was something along the lines of, 'Good luck for the race, we want you to win for Ayrton and win the championship. In Ayrton's absence, we are right behind you.'

I went into the Williams motorhome and looked at a picture of Ayrton on the wall. It brought back memories of the distress and emotion at his funeral, and the huge sense of loss in Brazil. When Brazil won the World Cup, the team – and the whole country – immediately paid tribute to Ayrton and now I felt that I could actually help those fans raise their spirits once more. I knew I could never be a patch on Ayrton but, nonetheless, I felt a responsibility to perform at my very best. I knew I really had to give it a go. It was a poignant moment but it gave me a very good feeling.

HEADING FOR SECOND PLACE

IN HUNGARY

Of course, I go into every Grand Prix utterly determined to do my best but there is something extra to be gained from having the importance of a particular race reinforced and lifted even further. It has something to do with winning other than just purely for yourself. A year before, I won my first Grand Prix in Hungary and, on that occasion, I got inspiration during the race by thinking of my father. I was not under serious pressure from the driver in second place but I knew I had to maintain concentration. I wanted to do well because it would have been something my father would have been really proud of. That was my spur in 1993 and, this time, I knew I would have to drive like never before to beat Schumacher. That's what made me feel good about this race.

This was the first time since Silverstone that we had been together on the front row and, in the light of what had happened there, it occurred to me that Michael might try to tempt me to overtake him during the parade lap. Sure enough, at one point on the back of the circuit, he braked very hard and slowed to a crawl. Of course, you could say that he was letting the field bunch up. But you might also say that he was trying to catch me out. Whatever his intention, I was not about to be tempted into an error. Indeed, I was just as interested in the fact that Michael seemed to be fairly wound up. Once or twice, he booted the throttle – and almost lost control. The car really stepped out of line and I began to realize he was quite tweaked up whereas I felt very relaxed, very comfortable.

Despite being on the dirty side of the track, I made a very good start, better than Michael, in fact. He reacted by edging across from the left and then jerking the wheel twice, trying to keep me on the right-hand side. I wasn't having any of that, so I returned the favour and he moved to the left and dropped back slightly. But the trouble was, I did not have enough momentum to get far enough ahead and sweep to the left in order to take the ideal line into the first right-hander. Michael passed me going through the corner – in fact, he came very close to the front of my car. I immediately thought of Katayama at Hockenheim. Above all, I wanted to be there at the finish of this race, so I let the Benetton go through and then gave chase.

Quite simply, we had not done the right thing in the race and Michael had stretched his points advantage

We both pushed very hard during the first two laps and, once again, he was ragged under pressure. I thought once again that everything was looking quite good. But after a few more laps, he settled down and began to pull away, at which point my fervent hope was that he was on a three-stop tactic and therefore running with a lighter load of fuel. If that was not the case and, like me, Michael was only going to stop twice, then we were in serious trouble.

As it turned out, my guess was correct and the Benetton pulled in after 17 laps. It was the perfect move because we were just about to hit heavy traffic and I got stuck in the middle of it, losing about 10 seconds in the process. Then I made my first stop as planned, came back out – and had to pass the same people all over again. It was an unnecessary loss of time, added to which, the Benetton tactic of running with a light load of fuel and reasonably fresh tyres meant Schumacher was able to deal more easily with the backmarkers. He was driving extremely well and there could be no denying that we were beaten fair and square.

I finished second, a good result. But a good result was not good enough and I was pretty annoyed when I got out of the car. I had driven well and got six points but, without wishing to sound ungrateful, that was not what I had wanted. Quite simply, we had not done the right thing in the race and Michael had stretched his points advantage back to 31. The appeal against his two-race ban had yet to be heard but, even assuming the penalty stood and I won the two races in question, I still needed to cut back an 11-point deficit. That meant beating Schumacher and Benetton in all of the remaining races. On the form we had seen in Hungary – and based on my feelings after the race – that did not seem likely.

On the other hand, I knew from experience that motor racing is not that straight-forward. By the time I was ready to travel to Belgium for the next race a fortnight later, I had picked myself up and was raring to go. I was ready to give Michael and every-one else a bit of a thrashing.

CHAPTER TEN
A QUESTION OF STATUS

THE BELGIAN AND ITALIAN GRANDS PRIX

The championship was turned completely on its head during the course of the Belgian and Italian Grands Prix. I was to score maximum points in both races – my primary objective in the first place, of course – but I had not anticipated yet another plunge into momentary despair, followed by a swift rise to elation in this extraordinary roller-coaster of a season.

I don't mind admitting that the disappointment of not winning in Hungary lingered into the days which followed. To my mind, that race had been crucial because we should – and could – have overturned Schumacher. The car felt good and we had given him a good race. But we hadn't won. I could see my championship chances evaporating.

I went to Spa-Francorchamps determined not to worry about the title, the sole aim being to win as many races as possible and let the championship take care of itself. In any case, Spa represented a good opportunity for us because the premium was on horsepower, an area in which Renault had the edge over Ford. But that did not take into account the notoriously uncooperative weather in this corner of the Ardennes.

There was much work to be done during practice, not least getting to grips with changes to the circuit, particularly at Eau Rouge. This is one of the most famous corners on any circuit in the world. It was similar to a ski-jump insofar as you rushed

down a hill towards the 'launch pad', which was the corner itself, a left–right–left which, in the middle, suddenly switched to a steep uphill section. You then crested the rise very quickly while turning left at the same time. It was an awesome corner, one which everyone liked. But there was not enough run-off area and the decision had been made to change the layout just for 1994. Sad, but it was a ruling which the GPDA felt was unavoidable.

Instead, we had a tight corner at the bottom of the hill, which slowed things down considerably. In addition, the track had been resurfaced in places, making it important to get out and discover the extent of the changes before the rain came. The track remained dry for about fifteen minutes on Friday morning. Then it rained, almost without ceasing, until just after the warm-up on Sunday morning.

There can be no denying that it is very dramatic to slide a car around in the wet but I always feel a little bit dejected when it rains

There is something about a wet race meeting which dampens the whole event in every sense. There can be no denying that it is very dramatic to slide a car around in the wet but I always feel a little bit dejected when it rains. It is as if this is not a proper event because you can't do your job to the full. At the end of the day, however, grid positions and results have the same value as anywhere else. But splashing round in the rain doesn't seem to be what you came for.

A wet practice session can throw up some interesting situations, particularly if the rain stops halfway through, as it did during first qualifying on Friday afternoon. The racing line will begin to dry out thanks to the cars displacing the water and you reach the point where it is time to change from wet, grooved tyres to slicks. Choosing the right moment is crucial, particularly if it comes towards the end of the session. You don't want to go onto dry tyres too soon and, at best, waste time slithering all over the place or, at worst, spinning off and damaging the car. On the other hand, you need to be ready for that moment when slicks become quicker on a drying track than wet tyres, especially if there are only a few minutes of practice remaining.

That was exactly what happened at Spa, but there was an added complication because of the changes to the track. As a rule of thumb, it is best to switch to slicks when the lap times have fallen to within about 10 seconds of a reasonable lap time in the dry. The only problem was, we had no idea of what a reasonable time should be on the revised circuit simply because there had been insufficient opportunity to build up speed during the brief period when the track was dry. Anywhere else, you could risk

THE BELGIAN GRAND PRIX

running slicks earlier than usual, but Spa is a different ball game entirely. For a start, the 4.3-mile track is the longest in use and conditions can vary dramatically from one part to the next. And then there is the thought that the lap average is 135 m.p.h. – and that includes a couple of very slow corners.

I decided that the best solution would be to stay out on wets. My lap times were coming down but, unbeknown to me, Rubens Barrichello and Schumacher had switched to slick tyres in order to try for a quick time right at the very end. I continued with wets – and I nearly got it right. Coming towards the end of what would be my quickest lap, I came across Schumacher, who was recovering after having spun off on his slicks! The Renault speed graph was to show that I lost half a second while backing off momentarily to avoid the Benetton – and that was the difference between my third place on the grid and pole position – which went to Barrichello.

That was a surprise to everyone as Rubens squeezed in a brave lap on slicks during the very last minutes of qualifying. It demonstrated how such practice sessions are a lottery. I don't think it's possible to judge scientifically whether or not the right decision has been made regarding tyres. Luck does play its part and, with final qualifying

DAVID BRABHAM IS ANOTHER
MOTOR RACING 'SON OF'.
I CAN SYMPATHIZE ENTIRELY

being washed out, the times established on Friday determined the grid positions. A Jordan was on pole for the first time.

Third place was reasonable under the circumstances. Barrichello would be directly ahead of me with Schumacher to the left, on the outside of the front row. There were many things to consider, not least being the fact that the first corner, a very tight hairpin, is notorious for creating havoc. I knew that Rubens would put up a strong fight to stay in front for as long as he could but my main concern was not to get stuck behind him, particularly going into the first corner, where Michael would have a clear run down the outside. So, with all that in mind, my thoughts before the start were preoccupied by the best way to tackle the first corner.

Throughout all of this, my team-mate kept pointing out that Rubens had a history of making poor starts in Formula 3 and Formula 3000. David continued with this theme right up to the point where we were about to leave the debrief room in the back of the transporter and prepare to go to the grid. He was saying things such as 'I'm really worried about the first corner,' or, 'How are you going to avoid a first corner accident?' Eventually, I simply said, 'Either you stop going on about the first corner, or I'm going to give you a slap.'

I was not sure if he was trying to wind me up but, either way, he had succeeded in doing just that. I didn't need to have a continual repetition of his fears concerning the start of the race. It may have been, of course, that David was merely talking about a point of common interest but this was at a time when I was trying to prepare myself positively for the race. You try to think in terms of not having an accident but he seemed to be harping on and on in a negative fashion and I had reacted to it. I did not mean for one second that I intended to have a punch-up but David was startled — as were the rest of the occupants of the debrief room — when I had a go at him and the whole thing turned into a bit of a moment. It was nothing personal, merely that David happened to be saying the wrong thing at the wrong time. I didn't know David that well and maybe I misunderstood him. Then again, maybe I didn't.

I knew that Rubens would put up a strong fight to stay in front for as long as he could

Anyway, I apologized to David after the race. I said that I had been completely out of order and we agreed to forget about it. Besides, by that stage, the race had given me plenty to think about in other directions.

In fact, there had been a great deal of serious discussion on the starting grid. The rain had stopped and the track was bone dry but, because of practice having been held in the wet, no one knew precisely the best set-up for their car for these more favourable conditions.

The pre-race countdown begins 30 minutes before the actual start time; in this case, 2 p.m. The pit lane remains open for 15 minutes, during which time a driver may complete as many laps as he wishes. But, because the grid area is rapidly filling with cars and people, the driver must pass through the pits each time he wants to do another lap. The trick in this instance was to squeeze in as many laps as possible in order to get a feel for the conditions and gather much-needed information on the car while, at the same time, trying to avoid being trapped in the pit lane after it had closed at 1.45 p.m. If that happens, a driver must start the race from the pit exit after the field has departed.

Our main concern was the so-called 'plank', a strip of wood attached to the underside of each car. This had been introduced for the German Grand Prix as a means of keeping the cars at a certain height above the ground at all times, thereby reducing the downforce generated and, as a result, cutting performance. The regulations made it quite clear that if, at the end of the race, the plank was worn by more than 1 millimetre anywhere along its length, then disqualification would follow.

Under normal circumstances, it was difficult enough making sure the car did not bottom excessively and grind away the plank. But, going into a race for which we had no experience at all of running the cars in dry conditions, this was a major concern. During the reconnaissance laps, I felt the car was bottoming too much. I asked to have it raised further off the ground, even though I knew that would reduce the overall performance. But the risk was not worth taking. I simply had to score as many points as I could and I was not prepared to have them taken away at the end of the race. Assuming, of course, I had safely negotiated the first corner . . .

In some ways, the start lived up to its reputation. The lights turned green – and immediately flicked back to red again. I went under the starting gantry wondering if the race was about to be stopped but, judging by Jean Alesi's furious pace as he stormed down the inside with the Ferrari's brakes locked as it brushed the barrier, the Belgian Grand Prix was definitely on. Mind you, I thought Alesi would almost cause the race to be stopped as he ran wide in the midst of the scramble through the hairpin. Fortunately, nobody hit the Ferrari and everyone made it through without incident – much to my relief, as you can probably appreciate.

I spent the first couple of laps feeling my way with the car, by which time Alesi had retired with engine trouble and Barrichello had dropped back. Michael was leading and I was second. This was going to be a very interesting comparison.

During our deliberations on the grid, I had decided to remove some of the wing angle in order to gain more speed on the straight. That now seemed like a wrong move because the car was not proving to be any faster; I could not exploit the potential extra speed because I did not have a high enough top gear to match. On top of this, the reduction in wing angle produced less downforce which, in turn, meant the car was not so quick in the twisty sections. It seemed I was losing out all round.

Michael had extended his lead to 16 seconds by the time we got to the pit stops. On the lap before I was due to come in, I was caught briefly behind a slower car at the Eau Rouge chicane. That allowed David, who had moved into third place on lap three, to close right up. I stopped first, David coming in a lap later. Schumacher had been in and out of the pits to retain his lead but David rejoined just in front of me. I knew straight away that this was not good news.

Schumacher had been in and out of the pits to retain his lead but David rejoined just in front of me. I knew straight away that this was not good news

David was racing with the knowledge that he would have to stand down in favour of Nigel Mansell for the last three races. With contracts for 1995 up for grabs, it was obvious that he was out to impress in the limited time he had available and earn himself a drive. It occurred to me that he might prove to be a little difficult to overtake. In actual fact, he was driving very quickly and very well. Occasionally, I would lose out in traffic but then I would pull it back. We were evenly matched and it was difficult for me to close right up. I didn't particularly want to race David because it made little sense. There seemed to be no point in having two drivers from the same team competing against each other when one of them really needed to go after the guy in the lead in order to improve his chances of winning the championship.

I got on the radio and told the team something along the lines that David was losing me time to Schumacher, by which I meant that if David moved over I could close the gap on the leader (which was now 10 seconds) during the remaining 12 laps or so.

The team said they understood but, when David did not make way, it was clear that no orders had been issued. Okay, I thought, if that's the way you want it then I'll just keep pushing and look for an opportunity to get by. A few times I got reasonably close, but not enough to have a stab which would guarantee success without jeopardizing us both. Then David suddenly pulled into the pits.

His rear wing had been drooping and vibrating quite badly on one side and he had been brought in as a precautionary measure to have it checked over. Nothing was seriously amiss and David was sent on his way again. Meanwhile, with the benefit of a clear road, I had set the fastest lap of the race and I was lapping half a second quicker than before. The difference that running in clean air made to the performance of the car was noticeable but, unfortunately, there were very few laps remaining and Schumacher was too far ahead.

Had I been able to move ahead of David a few laps earlier, I could have got to within striking distance of the Benetton

I was not amused because, had I been able to move ahead of David a few laps earlier, I could have got to within striking distance of the Benetton. Whether I would have been able to take the lead is another matter but my mood was not helped when I discovered that Michael had spun earlier in the race. He admitted later that he had made the mistake because he was running close to the limit and that left me wondering what might have happened if I had been able to push him even harder.

I told Frank Williams and Patrick Head that I thought they had made a wrong decision in not telling David to let me through. They obviously did not agree. I was bemused by their approach because, apart from the fact that credit should be given to the driver who is fighting for the championship, the follow-on logic was that if they didn't accept what I was saying then they did not have faith in their Number One driver. And, if that was the case, then it undermined everything I was trying to do.

It meant I had to think very hard about where I actually stood within the team. On the one hand, it seemed they wanted me to do the job of Number One driver but, on the other, they were not prepared to credit me with the authority to behave like one and get the job done. That was a blow; a bit of a shock to the system.

I had plenty of time to mull this over during a three-hour crawl to Brussels airport. Apart from coping with unbelievable traffic, I wasn't happy with this latest turn of events and I was giving serious thought to my future with the team. I didn't want to be either taken for granted or patronized. I wanted to be respected for what I was doing rather than simply being tolerated. And the fact that I missed the turn-off to the airport and had to dash into the terminal hardly improved my frame of mind.

I sought the peace and quiet of the airport lounge, where I could meditate on things and get over my disappointment when, to my surprise, Ann Bradshaw, the team's press officer, came rushing over and said, 'Congratulations – you've won the race!' I was in no mood for jokes and it was not until Ann explained that Schumacher's car had been declared illegal that the truth began to sink in. At post-race scrutineering, the plank on the Benetton had been worn away by more than the permitted 1 millimetre. There was no question about it: he was out and I had won. Instead of scoring maximum points, Schumacher had none. And I now had 10 points instead of 6. It didn't take Einstein to work out that I was back in with a chance since we had also reached the start of Schumacher's two-race ban.

In some ways, the disqualification was tough on Michael because, as I explained earlier, that sort of thing could happen to anyone. The plank is easily worn out when you have a car with two or three tonnes of downforce acting on it while negotiating the kind of bumps to be found on any race track. Schumacher claimed that his plank had been worn when he spun across a kerb but that did not wash at all because only the rear of the Benetton had hit the kerb whereas the worn area was in the centre of the car.

The point was that if the car had been run low enough to wear away the plank to that degree then, almost certainly, there was a performance advantage to be had – perhaps enough to make the difference between our lap times. It could be argued that his car was faster purely because it was running illegally. The first legal car to reach the finish was my Williams-Renault. So I won the race. End of story.

EDUCATING THE BOYS IN
THE ANCIENT ART OF SEGA'S
COMPUTER RACING

Between leaving the race track and reaching home that evening, the championship had taken on an entirely different look. From being more or less a lost cause, it was suddenly a viable proposition. From having quietly sipped nothing stronger than tea immediately after the race, it was a case of walking into the house later that evening and opening a bottle of champagne. I don't mind admitting, my mood had changed dramatically. And it was very nice to sit down in my own front room and quietly begin to untangle my mixed emotions.

Even after the most disappointing weekend, I find great comfort in returning home and suddenly switching back to family life. Some people say that the ideal way to be a racing driver is to remain single. Certainly, that is true – but only if your life is totally devoted to racing and absolutely nothing else matters. It isn't like that in my case.

My father had been a Grand Prix driver for two years when I was born so, obviously, I grew up knowing very little else. As far as I was concerned, he was a fine example of how it was possible to be a driver and have a family. Enzo Ferrari once said that a driver with children is a second a lap slower than one without. I think that has been completely disproved; Nigel Mansell is the perfect example in recent years. My father went on record as saying that it was a good idea for drivers to have families because it gave them stability; a firm foundation in a shifting environment. If you have a family, you always know that it is there to come back to and that can be very important when motor racing makes a driver feel insecure and vulnerable. Although he was unmarried, even Ayrton gained strength from his family and close friends.

It sounds extremely callous to say that you are going to have a family purely as a means of improving your career chances! But these things do go hand-in-hand and it is perhaps no coincidence that, in my case, starting a family and becoming more dedicated as a driver should have occurred at the same time. Until then, I had few responsibilities. I could survive, take care of myself on very little money and I would be the only person to suffer as a consequence of my own actions. I thought I was being professional and totally focused then, but realize now how undisciplined I was. All of that changes when you have a family.

Georgie and I were married in 1988. At the time, I was doing very little driving but when we had Oliver the following year, the fact that he was handicapped changed my outlook on many aspects of life. It brought it home to me that I was fortunate to be able to drive racing cars for a living at all. Georgie and Oliver were extremely important to me and it became clear that, if I was going to race in order to earn a living, then I had better not waste any opportunities. It was not a case of

CLOCKWISE FROM ABOVE:
SANDY HILL. IMPORTANT PRE-
SEASON TRAINING IN ANTIGUA . . .

CHRISTENING A ROWING BOAT
DOES NOT ENTAIL SMASHING A
BOTTLE OF CHAMPAGNE OVER ITS
BOW, FOR OBVIOUS REASONS

SPEED SPORTS ARE COMPULSORY
FOR RACING DRIVERS ON HOLIDAY

THE RENAULT ACTUALLY GETS
WASHED (BY MY SON, OF COURSE)

having squandered my chances unnecessarily in the past; it was just that the complexion of the whole thing had changed. And changed for the better. I discovered that I could cope with getting up at 3 a.m. to feed Oliver, lose sleep and yet still drive racing cars. It taught me that I could function on a lot less sleep than I had previously thought necessary. Indeed, life actually started to look up from a career point of view around this time too.

The down side, however, is that as things get better and better, I find I spend less time at home and that makes it seem even more valuable than before. I fight very hard to create time with the family. It is not enough to have one day here and one day there. If I have been at a race for four days and return late on Sunday night, the children go to school the following day and, by the time they

return, they are off the clock with excitement and it is very hard to relax with them. After spending two or three days together as a family, they begin to calm down. I can be a normal person with them again and they start to accept my presence rather than becoming worried that, every time I leave the room, I am going to jet off once more. Returning home and immediately becoming a family man is not a problem in itself. It is the adjustment back and forth which creates the difficulty.

Being with the family brings a driver back to reality. Although I did not have much chance to get to know Ayrton very well, it was noticeable that he appreciated more and more the pleasures which came with returning home to Brazil. I remember talking to him at a test in Spain, just before we went to the Pacific Grand Prix. He had been in Grand Prix racing for ten years and it was apparent that the appeal of travelling to Europe and driving Grand Prix cars was definitely on the wane. He struck me as quite a lonely bloke at the races and yet, for a long time, Formula One had meant everything to him.

In my view, racing should not be the only thing in a driver's life. There is absolutely no reason why a driver should perform any better if he has no outside interests whatsoever. If he thinks and breathes motor racing to the exclusion of all else, I do not believe that it makes a driver more effective. In fact, I think it can make him more vulnerable because such total devotion creates its own pressures. It is no good being so obsessed with winning that life becomes completely meaningless if you don't finish first. Winning a race is a very transient thing. Once it's done, it's done. It does not carry you through the rest of your life. That said, my mind was firmly focused on winning the Italian Grand Prix as I packed my bags for the race at Monza on 11 September.

I had taken a fairly momentous decision during the previous week by asking to change my engineer for the rest of the season. Ever since I started racing with Williams in 1993, I had worked with John Russell who, prior to me, was Riccardo Patrese's

YOUR NAME IN LIGHTS.

THE SCOREBOARD, A FAMOUS

MONZA LANDMARK

engineer. There had been absolutely no problem between us. My thinking went back to the change within the team following the loss of Senna at Imola. At the time, I had said to Frank that they should be confident in counting on me as their Number One driver, and that I should work with the Number One engineer, David Brown, and the Number One engineer from Renault; in effect, the people who had worked on Ayrton's car. This was the same team which had worked with Alain Prost in 1993 and Nigel Mansell two years before that. I believed the change would be significant because it would be proof of Frank's commitment to me. It would help me feel confident about tackling the task of leading the attack for Williams-Renault. In fact, I thought he would be reassured by my belief that I could carry the weight of responsibility for the team's fortunes for the remainder of the year.

The switch was never made because, I think, they knew Nigel was coming back for the French Grand Prix and he would want to work with David. Fair enough. Frank had made his decision and I was happy to get on with things as they were. There was

no reason to believe that I could not get the job done with John (to whom I felt a great deal of loyalty in any case). Indeed, we did just that, to the point where I was in with a chance of winning the championship. I never had any doubts about John's ability as an engineer.

But events at Spa had made me unsure about the team's feelings towards me. Contract time was approaching and I felt, at the time, that I did not want to stay with a team which was not giving me their backing. I might have been completely wrong to think that but the net effect was to make me dig my heels in and ask for what I wanted. And I wanted to work with David Brown. I felt that, apart from the reasons already stated, after eighteen months spent working with John, it would be good to get a fresh perspective on things and widen my view of the whole scene. It also challenged my own self-confidence at a crucial time by raising the stakes a little since failure to perform with David could be regarded as a miscalculation on my part. But the way I saw it was that I was fighting for the championship and I wanted to do whatever was necessary for my peace of mind. If that's what was required to enable me to do the job, then so be it. I shouldn't have to give an explanation for it. When I told Patrick that this was what I wanted, he stressed the point that it was not going to be a popular move. I said I understood, but this was the way I felt – so let's do it.

From where I was sitting on the second row of the grid, beating the Ferraris was not going to be a simple matter

I dreaded arriving at Monza. I knew I had ruffled a few feathers in the team and that it would cause an atmosphere. It was particularly difficult to greet John because, despite trying to reach him by telephone, we hadn't actually spoken since the decision had been made. I said very briefly that I understood he must be extremely upset, but that this was a move I had wanted to make. I couldn't really offer any explanation other than to say thank you very much for everything in the past. It was hardly a satisfactory moment for either of us.

From my point of view, the change did have the desired effect because it made me concentrate even more on the job in hand and I found I was in the right frame of mind for driving. There were distractions outside the car because I was continuing to think about the options available to me for 1995 and, to that end, I had brought along my solicitor to talk to various people.

Despite Schumacher's absence, my job was to beat the Ferrari drivers, who just seemed to get stronger and stronger as the weekend progressed. Monza is all about horsepower and Ferrari seemed to have an abundant supply, so much so that the red cars filled the front row at home for the first time in nineteen years. People had been saying, almost matter-of-factly, that because of Michael's ban, all I had to do was win in Italy and in Portugal and the gap between us would be just one point. But, from where I was sitting on the second row of the grid, beating the Ferraris was not going to be a simple matter. If anything, the easy assumption that I would win was actually increasing the pressure.

As if that was not enough, I ran into all sorts of niggling problems before the race had even started. Trouble with the throttle meant I was unable to complete all I had wanted to do during the warm-up on race morning. Then, when I left the pit lane to make my way to the grid, the car developed a severe brake judder. I returned to the pits and they told me to do another lap to see if the problem got any worse.

In fact, it disappeared and the car felt very good; really very good indeed.

Sometimes you get a slightly hysterical feeling as you go to the grid, a feeling which says, 'This car is really good and I can do something with it.' I was quietly suppressing a smile as I made my way towards the front of the grid but the feeling of smug satisfaction changed dramatically when I climbed from the car and saw oil pouring onto the track.

As I stood there, watching the mechanics try to fix the leak, Patrick was saying that I may have to run back to the garage and get into the spare car and Bernie Ecclestone, in the midst of a scrum of television cameras and photographers, came over and said, 'Meet Sylvester Stallone.' We managed to have a few words in the thick of this hubbub and then, suddenly, I was told to leg it down the pit lane. Sod's law decreed that the Williams garage should be at the far end, which meant a dash of 300 yards and more. And the pit lane was about to close. So much for feeling good about doing well in this race.

I climbed into the spare car. There was no time to put on my crash helmet properly and I just sat on my gloves. All I wanted to do was get out of the garage before they closed the pit lane. Then there was an argument about whether or not I could actually leave the pits because it is not permitted to have two cars on the grid. The team had to decide whether or not they could fix my race car and, if they couldn't, whether they could actually remove it from the grid in time to let me out in the spare car.

Eventually I was told 'Go! Go!' I got to the end of the pit lane with about a minute

to spare – and the official would not let me out. The clock was ticking away and you can't keep the engine running for a long time while the car is stationary. If I was going to be forced to start the race from the pit lane, I could kiss goodbye to the race, the championship, the lot! And if I was to sit there much longer with the engine getting hotter and hotter, I was not going to be able to motor anywhere. So, I banged the car in gear and drove off! I quickly realized that this car felt nowhere near as good as my race car and in addition it had not got the uprated RS6C engine. I returned to the grid a lot less happy this time round. Talk about rapidly changing fortunes in motor racing.

On that subject, one of the surprises of practice had been a revival by Lotus, Johnny Herbert qualifying fourth to start alongside me on the second row, his previous best this season having been fifteenth on the grid in Germany. He made the most of his new-found competitiveness by getting off the line very quickly. Johnny was alongside as we went towards the first corner and I was on the point of conceding it to him when the picture changed completely yet again.

Eddie Irvine had made a very fast start from the fifth row and the first I was aware of it was when a green and blue car streaked through on my right and slammed into the back of the Lotus. The impact spun Johnny round and he was broadside, directly ahead of me, on the narrowest part of the track with twenty-two cars bearing down on

MONZA IS MOSTLY CHICANES AND LONG STRAIGHTS. THE REAR WING IS SMALL AND AT A SHALLOW ANGLE TO EXPLOIT THE ADVANTAGE OF SPEED ON THE STRAIGHTS

A WONDERFUL SIGHT: A RED
FERRARI LEADING AT MONZA.
FORTUNATELY, IT DIDN'T
LAST LONG . . .

us. I managed to scrape through but the chaos which followed meant the race had to be stopped.

David had been an innocent victim and he returned to the pits on foot, looking for the back-up, which was, of course, my repaired race car. In fact, I was asked if I wanted to return to it but, even though the one I was in did not feel as good, I had a gut feeling about the race car. There had been a number of small problems with that car all weekend and I wasn't sure about it. Besides, the spare car was being attended to by the self-styled 'Floyds', a good bunch of guys who had worked on my winning car throughout 1993 and up to Silverstone. I felt the right thing to do was stay with this car although, with time running out and the team eager to have one car tailored to suit David, I did not really have much choice.

This time, the start was incident-free, with Alesi pulling clear from Berger and me. He opened a gap of about 14 seconds but failed to get any further. This was good news because, if Alesi was going to stop twice, then the margin would not be enough when it came to taking an advantage over the one-stop strategy I had chosen. All of that became academic when Alesi failed to rejoin after his gearbox had broken while he made his pit stop – although it would be some time before I would realize he was out of the race – and I closed right up on Berger who, like me, was intending to stop just once.

In fact, Gerhard was to be delayed by another car in the pit lane but, regardless of that, my lap times had been quicker in and out of the pits and I would have taken the lead in any case. Or so I thought. After the pit stops, I was indeed ahead of the Ferrari but I was rather surprised to find myself in second place, behind my team-mate. I could only guess that his actual stop had been fractionally quicker but, whatever the

reason, I was directly behind David, but even closer than we had been at Spa. This time, however, he was asked to move over and I took the lead. Then it was a simple matter of maintaining station until the end of the race. If only motor racing was that straightforward!

While following the Ferrari, I had been covered in oil, a glutinous mess which was simply impossible to remove. It was all over my mirrors and it seemed to melt my visor.

Certainly, I could not wipe it clean and I could barely see where I was going. On top of this, I was having trouble with a type of pelmet or bib which I had fitted to the bottom of my helmet. The intention was, in the event of a spillage during a pit stop, to stop fuel from going inside my helmet. But the trouble was, this cloth bib was actually restricting the air flow and my struggle with the oil was made worse by a visor which began to mist on the inside. Having run out of the throw-away visor rip-offs, I was spending my time attempting to clean the visor itself while fighting with this bib and attempting to tear it off in order to allow the passage of air inside the helmet. I was grateful for David's presence directly behind me, even though Berger was more than 10 seconds further back.

During the final laps, I remembered the previous year when I was dutifully fol-lowing Alain at the head of the field, only to witness at first hand the engine failure which robbed him of victory. I was desperately anxious that the same thing should not happen to me and I backed off on the straights in order to avoid stressing the engine any more than was necessary. Then I had a radio message to say that Berger was on a final charge and the Ferrari was only six seconds behind. Even so, I knew David and I had everything under control and I was thinking how wonderful a one-two finish would be for everyone on the team.

As I crossed the line, I thought, 'Brilliant! We've done it!' Then I looked in my mirrors for David. There happened to be a Ligier directly behind me on the road but, because my mirrors were so blurred with oil, I couldn't quite make out who it was. I thought it was David. It was not until I reached the final corner on my slowing down lap that I saw David's car parked on the grass. He had run out of fuel – in what had been my original race car.

That meant Berger had finished second, with Mika Hakkinen third for McLaren. Gerhard had suffered a massive accident during the morning warm-up and, when we reached the finish, he was so stiff he could hardly raise his head. It had been a very brave performance because, clearly, he had been in a lot of pain. But I knew from my experience the previous year, when Alesi had finished second for Ferrari, that the reception from the crowd would provide the perfect cure for Gerhard's discomfort.

While we were climbing the rostrum, I said to Mika, 'You won't believe this; just wait and see!' Sure enough, we walked onto the podium and there was a roar which was deafening. The reception at Monza is absolutely brilliant. There is no equal to it and it really sums up what Grand Prix racing is all about. It also brings home the importance of Ferrari, not just in Italy, but in Formula 1 as a whole.

Monza was difficult for many reasons: I had to win; the Ferraris were very competitive; I was driving the spare car which handled badly due to a misunderstanding over the correct set-up; the engine was not up to our latest specification and had the wrong engine mapping (ie: fuel/ air/ ignition timing programme) which was a mistake due to the swapping of cars on the grid. And I was having visibility problems. Nevertheless, I won the race by setting the fastest lap when Berger was in the pits, thereby overtaking him and controlling the pace of the race without overstressing the car and engine. I felt it was one of my most satisfying races; one I was proud of; one where I felt like a Grand Prix driver capable of using his head to win. This was not one from the heart, perhaps, but it felt mighty good and now I was only 11 points behind Michael.

CHAPTER ELEVEN

UPSIDE-DOWN

THE PORTUGUESE AND EUROPEAN GRANDS PRIX

GERHARD BERGER —
'ACCIDENT-ALLY' IN THE WAY
DURING PRACTICE IN PORTUGAL

During the days following the race in Italy, I discovered that there was criticism from some quarters concerning my performance at Monza. One or two people had hoped for a sort of gung-ho approach to the weekend and were disappointed when I failed to live up to their expectations. Everyone wants to see an exciting race — I can understand that — but I wasn't going to be pushed into providing entertainment just for the sake of it. I had nothing to gain from that tactic either at Monza or in the next race at Estoril. My aim was to make the most of Schumacher's absence and score maximum points.

I went to Portugal knowing that, on the one hand, I wanted to be assertive and start the build-up for Michael's return in Spain. On the other hand, I knew there was no need to extend myself unnecessarily because it was clear that I had a car capable of winning the Portuguese Grand Prix. I knew we would be stronger than Ferrari and I really thought it was simply a matter of getting the job done. My approach was one of resisting the pressure to do something which I felt the occasion did not demand. If that failed to meet the requirements of certain observers, then that was just too bad.

None the less, I was aware of the need to establish superiority during qualifying. On the first day, things were going according to plan until Gerhard Berger put in an amazing performance to claim pole. His timing was excellent because the weather on Friday was cooler than it would be the following day; the track was therefore at its best when he set his time. It was even more impressive because of the fact that he was never able to get close to that lap time again at any stage during the weekend. Regardless of how he did it, Berger had established the benchmark and my attempts to get close were frustrated for a variety of reasons, one of which was very spectacular.

Going off line to avoid a Simtek during my qualifying run cost me about three-tenths of a second on a lap which otherwise would have been good enough for pole. Then, just after Berger had set his best time, I came across the Ferrari at a very slow part of the circuit. Gerhard was going at the sort of pace which said he was not going to move out of the way but, at the same time, he was going just slow enough to mess up my lap.

It was a rather unsubtle piece of blocking and there was a temptation to become frustrated. I had to guard against that because it is easy to make a mistake during qualifying and have an accident which can affect not just practice but the race itself. Nigel Mansell was in with a chance of winning the 1987 championship when he crashed during practice in Japan, the penultimate round of the series. That accident put him out for the rest of the season, so my approach was one of self-preservation and caution because I did not want to ruin my chance of closing the gap on Schumacher. But even the best laid plans are at the mercy of fate – as I was about to find out.

I was on my very last lap and it seemed like a good one until I caught Eddie Irvine in the Jordan

I was on my very last lap and it seemed like a good one until I caught Eddie Irvine in the Jordan. With the session nearing its end, it was obvious that Eddie was probably on his last lap too when he didn't move out of the way. I knew this was going to cost me a bit of time as we entered the same tight piece of track where I had previously been held up by Berger. This was actually a section of the circuit which had been revised as another GPDA safety measure, a part of the track which I referred to as Cadwell Park because of its similarity to the very, very tight and twisty circuit in Lincolnshire where I used to race motor bikes. In fact, the alterations were out of keeping with the rest of Estoril but it was to turn out quite well during the race. Practice, though, would be a different matter entirely.

Going into this new section, Eddie lost control of his car and started heading towards the barriers. Since I was fully committed to my fast lap, and it seemed Eddie was going to make a quick exit somewhere on my left, I kept my foot on the throttle. But he half-caught the car and spun back on to the track. By this time, I was ahead of the Jordan but hard on the brakes and changing down to first gear for the slowest cor-

QUICK ESCAPE FROM THE

WRECKAGE

ner on the circuit. I could sense he was coming towards me and I stayed as far right as I could in the hope that he would whiz past, straight into the gravel trap on the outside of the corner. In actual fact, he reversed into the left-hand side of my car and my rear wheel rode over his. In an instant, my car was flipped high into the air.

I didn't have time to be frightened even though I could feel that the contact between the two tyres had given the car plenty of rotation. In fact, I thought it might go right round and land on its wheels again. I had never, ever, been upside-down in a car of any sort but, as drivers involved in accidents usually say, it seemed to happen in slow motion. That was particularly so because, having been in the middle of a qualifying lap, I was concentrating so hard that I was able to think about each stage of the accident and attempt to work out what the consequences might be.

It was very much like doing aerobatics in an aeroplane, an experience I was familiar with, although I quickly realized this was not the sort of thing I wanted to do too often in a racing car. The car had flipped off the track itself and I knew I was going to land upside-down. My main concern was having the roll hoop above the back of my head bury itself in the

I didn't blame Eddie for my predicament; it wasn't his fault because he obviously didn't mean to hit me

gravel, thus leaving my head and neck to take the load. Fortunately, the roll hoop, rising behind my head and designed specifically for accidents such as this, fully supported the car, which was a relief because one of my concerns had been the thought of fuel leaking from the valve used for quick refuelling during pit stops. Had the car sunk into the gravel, there was always the risk that the fuel valve would be depressed.

That aspect had worried me right from the start of the season when the arrival of refuelling had meant the introduction of valves which you could push open with one finger. That was all very well when the car was upright and it was necessary to make a quick connection during the pit stops. But if the car was upside-down and deep enough in the gravel to have the valve pressed open, then the chances were that the driver would be trapped in the cockpit as fuel leaked from the tank.

In this case, it was what you might call a trouble-free accident insofar as there was no fuel leak and I was able to get out of the cockpit in a matter of seconds. I remember turning off the electrics and the engine and then recalling the fact that, in many cases, the most serious damage is done when a driver, in his anxiety to get out of an inverted car, undoes his seat belts in the usual way – and falls on his head. I put one hand on to the ground in order to support myself when I released the buckle and I was able to slide out of the cockpit with no drama at all.

I jumped over the crash barrier, where Irvine was waiting. He seemed to be in a worse state than me because this was the last thing he needed. Eddie had been involved in a number of incidents, either through his own fault or through back luck. And now he had guaranteed the headlines once again by putting one of the championship contenders out of qualifying in a pretty spectacular fashion. I didn't blame Eddie for my predicament; it wasn't his fault because he obviously didn't mean to hit me.

It was just unfortunate that he happened to lose control of his car at that precise moment.

My over-riding feeling was one of relief. I wasn't upset about failing to get pole position because the important thing was that I had managed to escape unharmed. I could tell that was also the feeling within the team because, when I arrived back in the garage, I was greeted by a sea of smiling faces. It had been a nerve-racking moment as they watched the incident on television and everyone was simply pleased to see that I was OK and walking about.

In fact, they were to become very angry when the car was finally returned in a bit of a state. The accident itself had done surprisingly little damage but I became aware of possible trouble as I watched the marshals trying to put the car back on its wheels. When it was on its side, I told them to let it down gently, not to drop it.

I may as well not have bothered because they simply gave it a push and the car smacked on to the ground. By this stage, the practice session had been stopped, so there was no urgency about getting the car out of harm's way. And yet they insist-

TO BE A MARSHAL IN PORTUGAL, YOU NEED TO BE ALERT, ABLE TO REACT QUICKLY AND POSSESS A KEEN INTEREST IN THE SPORT

NOT AS BAD AS IT LOOKS.
I AM ACTUALLY ON THE TRACK
AND NOT PLOUGHING THROUGH
THE GRAVEL

ed on attaching a tow-rope to the front suspension (rather than using the recommended towing point in the roll hoop) and then dragged the car across the gravel at about 30 m.p.h. In so doing, they managed to tear the suspension mounting away from the chassis and damage the bodywork and various bits and pieces.

The net result was a car which, apart from the chassis and the gearbox, was a write-off. Because the car had been upside down while the engine was running, the oil had fallen out of the sump, so, the engine had to be changed, along with all of the suspension, wings and bodywork. It was a complete rebuild which meant my mechanics had to work all night. But, in the end, the car was fine and I was completely unhurt. It was a miraculous escape and it did not put me off in the slightest because I was already thinking about the job which had to be done on Sunday.

As I mentioned earlier, the track conditions were less favourable during final qualifying and, even though David and I were among the few drivers to go quicker than we had on the first day, we could not dislodge Berger from pole. None the less, I would be starting from the front row and that seemed reasonable enough.

In fact, I was more concerned about David than I was about Berger. I felt the Williams car was better than the Ferrari and, even if Gerhard made a faster start, there was every chance I could stay with him and watch his every move. David would not be so predictable because this was going to be his last race prior to Nigel Mansell's return for the final three Grands Prix. I knew it would be in the team's best interest to guarantee that I finished ahead of David but the fact remained that he did not, at that point, have a firm offer of a drive with Williams in 1995. He was starting the Portuguese Grand Prix from third place on the grid and he had a car which was capable of winning. I could understand his dilemma: should he do his own thing and try to win or should he play the game and finish second, content in the knowledge that he had done a good job for the team? It was a difficult question.

Having been in exactly the same position with Alain Prost in 1993, I knew that being asked to finish second goes against a racing driver's instincts. I was slightly uncertain about what David would choose to do but, in the end, I decided that it made little difference because I had to win the race

Berger sped away from pole and David tucked in behind the Ferrari. I knew, with 71 laps to go, I would need to be patient

in any case in order to keep my championship hopes alive. None the less, while I felt I could beat David, I knew he was getting better all the time. I would need to stay on my toes right from the start. That plan went awry seconds before the lights turned green.

Each driver is supposed to line up inside an area defined by a white line painted on the grid. Because the car is not permitted to cross the front of its respective box before the start, I usually stop short of the white line at the front in order to allow some leeway in case the car creeps forward. In this case, the red lights had come on and, as I engaged the clutch to the point where it began to bite, the car started to move — and the lights seemed to be staying red for ever. Of course, the very second I stopped the car rolling, the lights changed to green.

Immediately, I was at a disadvantage as Berger sped away from pole and David tucked in behind the Ferrari. I knew, with 71 laps to go, I would need to be patient. Such a theory is all very well but I was dismayed to find that, while the car was good on 90 per cent of the circuit, the traction was so poor coming out of the new hairpin that I was losing a huge amount of time. I tried as best I could to stay with the leaders but, clearly, the set-up of my car was less than perfect. I got on the radio, briefly explained the problem and suggested there may be something wrong with the tyre pressures. Obviously, there was nothing they could do in the short term but maybe adjustments could be made to the set of tyres I was due to take on at the first pit stop.

In the mean time, Berger had disappeared with gearbox trouble. It was then a matter of getting to the finish but I did not want David to continue pulling away from me. At one point, his lead stretched to six seconds and there was nothing I could do

THINGS LOOKING UP AT ESTORIL

about it. It was annoying, to say the least, but there was no point in becoming irritated because that can be a recipe for allowing competitive ego to push too hard and prompt a driving error. I simply had to hang on and wait for the first pit stop.

I refuelled and changed tyres at the end of lap 19. Instantly, the car felt better. I began to close on David and, when he got caught behind some back-markers, I was right with him as we went into the revised section of track.

I had raised the subject of this corner at the drivers' briefing earlier in the day. In my view, it could be a potential hazard, particularly when the field was tightly bunched during the first few laps. In order to get round the corner, it is necessary to go very wide on the way in. It seemed to me that the temptation to dive down the inside would be too much on the opening lap and there was every chance that two cars could become tangled and block the track at its narrowest point, in which case, there would be no alternative but to stop the race. I suggested that there should be a yellow (no overtaking) flag displayed at that corner for the first lap. Roland Bruynseraede, the FIA safety delegate, agreed but, to my surprise, one or two drivers suggested that the yellow flag should be there for the whole race. I have to admit that I thought it was a sensible idea although, just as I closed in on David, I was glad the full-race yellow had not been approved.

A few laps earlier, someone had gone off at the hairpin and sprayed gravel on to the track. People were going round on the outside in order to avoid the small pebbles. My momentum was such that now was the time to overtake and, when David steered clear of the gravel, I dived down the inside and left him with no alternative but to let me through. The problem was, I was not entirely sure if I could actually make it round the corner from such a tight angle. I had a feeling it would be possible to scrabble round but, having pointed out the hazards of this corner at the briefing, I was in danger of finding myself in a very embarrassing position in every sense.

I managed it and, once into the lead, I was able to pull away and take command of the race. Jean Alesi was about fifteen seconds behind in third place but, when the Ferrari tangled with a back-marker and retired, that left Mika Hakkinen a further 10 seconds in arrears. My only concern now was a mechanical problem robbing me of those 10 points.

I eased off in the closing stages, allowing David to close in and emphasize the first one-two for Williams since the French Grand Prix in July 1993. When it came to historical facts, it was intriguing to note that this was the first one-two for British drivers since 1969 when my father won the Monaco Grand Prix and Piers Courage finished second in a Brabham – entered by Frank Williams.

Statistical quirks aside, this was a very, very satisfying result for the whole team. Apart from the obvious pleasure of having achieved what I had set out to do, it was very heartening to see David finally make it to the podium after some pretty grim luck during the previous two races. I felt particularly pleased for the guys who worked on his car because they had been through an extremely tough season with nothing to show for it. It was like the end of a drought.

All told, this was a fulfilling result for Williams, Renault and Rothmans and its importance could not be underestimated. We had established ourselves as a major force just as Schumacher was about to return and continue his fight for the championship.

A VERY HAPPY WILLIAMS TEAM GREET DAVID AND ME ON OUR ARRIVAL IN PARC FERME. THE FIRST ONE-TWO FOR WILLIAMS-RENAULT SINCE JULY 1993

HANDS-ON MANAGEMENT.
THE MOST IMPORTANT BIT OF THE
CAR, AS FAR AS I'M CONCERNED.
THE DETACHABLE STEERING
WHEEL (REMOVED FOR EASIER
COCKPIT ACCESS AND EXIT)
OBVIOUSLY CONTROLS THE
DIRECTION AND ALLOWS ME TO
BALANCE THE CAR WHILE SLIDING,
AS WELL AS PROVIDING THE
CONTROLS FOR CHANGING GEAR

Coming out of the last corner, with the finishing line in sight, I had got on the radio and said, 'Here I come!' Not only did I mean I was about to take the flag, I was also saying we were on the move and about to put the squeeze on Schumacher and Benetton. There were lots of cheers and everyone was hugging each other and being very un-British by showing bags of emotion. I got on the radio again and said, 'I can't believe it! One point behind Michael. Yes!'

It was a huge release as far as I was concerned. I had reckoned before these two races that the statistical chances of pulling off a pair of straight wins were not good. I felt it was no more than fifty-fifty because of the need to count on such a high degree of reliability and lack of incidents which could cause retirement through no fault of my own. But we had managed it. It was a hurdle which had, on paper, seemed easy. But the innocuous ones are always the most difficult to overcome.

An added bonus was the fact that I did not have to rush off in the usual manner immediately after the race. We were due to test at Estoril, starting on the following Tuesday. That meant I was able to celebrate in a night club on Sunday night and savour this win in a proper manner. Monday was spent playing golf (something which is usually hard to find time to do) and getting myself ready for testing knowing that Schumacher would be back in harness, preparing for the final three races which started in three weeks' time at Jerez in Spain.

There was quite a bit of needle between Williams and Benetton during the

A CLEAN SET OF WHEELS.
SCHUMACHER'S TYRES AND
WHEELS ARE PREPARED
FOR TESTING

three-day test. I was very keen to work on improving our car but, at the same time, I knew that it was not good to let Michael get away, even during testing. I wanted to put the onus on Schumacher to prove his speed. In some ways, I would have to work harder than him because, having already gone through qualifying and a Grand Prix at Estoril, it is possible to get a bit fed up after 200 laps of the same circuit. I wouldn't say the laps during testing were as intense as those during the race weekend, but this is fairly normal. I was actually more intent on working on the car than engaging in any psychological battle. Schumacher, on the other hand, was out to show that he had lost none of his speed during the enforced lay-off.

Matters were confused slightly by the track being even faster than it had been during practice for the Grand Prix. That sort of phenomenon is actually quite common and it is something we have to take into account when going for a quick lap during qualifying. In fact, changing track conditions are just one part of the complex discipline of qualifying which I don't think is fully understood by most Formula One fans.

COMING OUT TO PLAY.
EDGING THE WILLIAMS-RENAULT
OUT OF THE GARAGE AND INTO
THE SUN-LIT PIT LANE AT JEREZ

As I mentioned briefly in Chapter 3, practice on each of the two days is split into a morning session, when the times do not count for grid positions, and an hour of qualifying each afternoon. A maximum of 23 laps is permitted in the morning while, during qualifying, each driver is limited to 12 laps, and that includes the laps spent leaving and re-entering the pits. So if, say, a driver plans to make two separate runs during qualifying, he is effectively limited to eight quick laps because four will be spent getting in and out of the pits. Of course, it is also possible to make three separate runs, in which case, the number of flying laps is restricted to two each time. Those options are always available and drivers are free to go at any time they like during the 60-minute session. Choosing the right moment is vitally important.

Lap times can vary, depending on the conditions. The most damaging factor of all is the amount of sunlight beating down on the track. No one is exactly sure how it happens but the amount of grip available – or, the way the tyres work on the track – diminishes in proportion to the amount of heat in the track surface. These factors must be borne in mind because if, say, the first day is overcast but the forecast promises sunshine for the rest of the weekend, then the track is probably going to be at its quickest on the first day.

Having said that, quite a few tracks get quicker with use. If the circuit is new, or it has laid dormant for several months, the surface will be dusty and that sticks to the tyres and reduces grip. Once the dust has gone and the racing line has been cleaned by the passage of cars, the gradual application of rubber gives the tyres something to stick to which, in turn, allows more rubber to be laid on the surface. These characteristics vary

THE PORTUGUESE GRAND PRIX

from circuit to circuit; in some cases, the reverse is true and the track is at its best early on. It is simply a matter of experience and learning to exploit the varying conditions.

We use new tyres because they have the greatest performance potential. Again, that can differ from circuit to circuit. At some, the tyres offer maximum grip during the first timed lap; on others, the third lap may produce the best performance. Much depends on the type of tyre produced by Goodyear for the circuit in question. It could be that they have brought along a hard-wearing compound because that particular track dishes out a lot of punishment to the rubber. But at somewhere like Monaco, a soft compound is more suitable because the street circuit is quite smooth and does not have the sort of high-speed corner which seriously affects tyre wear.

Either way, the teams do not have any choice in the matter. We are given seven sets of whatever Goodyear think is best and we must make those 28 tyres last through all of practice and the race. That, too, presents a problem. The driver is torn between using his tyres to set a fast lap during qualifying and yet still having tyres which will be good during the race. It may be that he will choose not to use up his allocation of new tyres during qualifying in order to save a completely fresh set – or sets – for the race. The permutations are endless and it is vitally important to make the right decisions.

Quite apart from that, the way you drive in qualifying is altogether different from the way you drive during the race. It is very important to get into the right frame of mind because, I don't care what anyone says, it is impossible to suddenly switch it on. It is necessary to have the right amount of adrenalin flowing, the right amount of aggression. Some drivers do this by sitting with their eyes closed before the start as they race through the lap in their head. A single qualifying lap is rather like the long jump, or the javelin, or playing a golf shot. It is a one-off event requiring a sudden burst.

It helps if there is something to spur the driver along. For example, when I had to stand on the sidelines while they fixed my gearbox during the final qualifying session in France, it made me very impatient and that is a good state of mind to be in for qualifying. It is a case of almost being out of your mind with desire to get in and drive the car. When they finally wave you out of the garage, it is like a compressed spring being released; like a greyhound seeing the hare go by and being totally pumped up the moment the trap flies open. That's the way it needs to be during qualifying because, with a limit on the number of laps, a driver must be ready to go as fast as he can at the start of the first timed lap.

Qualifying is the peak of the driving experience because you rarely reach that level of commitment during a race

If, say, you are limited to two quick laps on your first run, it is necessary to go to the limit of your ability on the first lap. It calls for a lot of risk and trust in your skill and aggression to carry you through. If you happen to make a mistake on that first lap, then there is scope to back off, wait for a clear track and give it one more try on your second lap in the hope that the tyres have not already passed their best.

Although you try to your maximum on every set of tyres, you probably drive to the absolute peak only on your last run. Inevitably, you learn from the previous runs and make adjustments to improve the car a fraction here and there. It could be that the Renault technicians will produce a speed graph which shows that you were a bit slower than before at one particular point. Bit by bit, you piece the ultimate lap together and you draw on that experience and knowledge during the last lap. It is during that final attempt that you actually drive to the point where most drivers get the most satisfaction. It is a case of not truly knowing whether the ideas you have in mind will work; the sort of thing which makes the hair on the back of your neck stand up. There is nothing like it for exhilaration and excitement.

Qualifying is the peak of the driving experience because you rarely reach that level of commitment during a race. Finishing is the important thing in the race; you can't afford to make a mistake. During qualifying, when you venture into unknown territory, mistakes are tolerated because it shows you are trying. In many ways, qualifying provides more fun than the race because you have very little to lose. The race is a different matter entirely. And the next one in Spain would be more important than ever, which is why everyone threw so much into the test sessions at Estoril.

The British press turned out in force, not only because the championship was heading towards an interesting climax but also thanks to the return of Nigel Mansell as he took David Coulthard's place for the last three races. During testing, there are periods of inactivity while the car is worked on and I took the opportunity to talk to the media – as did Michael Schumacher. When we reached Jerez at the end of the week for the start of practice, I found out exactly what Michael had said.

He had come out with a few remarks which were quite obviously aimed in my direction with a view to running me down in the eyes of whoever cared to believe what he was saying. Apart from some rather personal and contentious statements, he said that if Ayrton was still alive, he would have been running rings around me.

I promptly went out and out-qualified Michael on Friday which, as you can imagine, was pretty sweet

I couldn't see the relevance in that and, in any case, I thought it was in very poor taste. I have enormous respect and admiration for Ayrton's abilities. I found the statement pretty hard to swallow, coming as it did from Michael because it was he who had blatantly set out to challenge Ayrton when he was alive and I think it's fair to say that there was precious little love lost between them. If such an outburst was meant to make me feel humble, then Michael had failed completely.

Apart from that, I did not think it was appropriate to start getting bitchy about each other at a time when we had a great opportunity to finish off the world championship in style; going racing without black flags, accusations of cheating and the various recriminations which had soured the sport during the previous months. This was going to be a straight, three-race battle and it seemed to me that the opportunity was being squandered by remarks which, at the time, I described as ill-advised, ill-conceived and immature. If Michael was trying to destabilize me, then he would have to do better than that.

I promptly went out and out-qualified him on Friday which, as you can imagine, was pretty sweet. To add insult to injury, Michael was also out-qualified by his girlfriend's ex-boyfriend and fellow German, Heinz-Harald Frentzen.

I didn't like it, but the controversy made life interesting because motor racing is not simply about what happens on the track. It can be theatrical at times, with propaganda and politics thrown in. At the end of the day, however, we all have to work together. In fact, there was a touch of irony that all of this should happen at Jerez

IT'S A SMALL WORLD.
AFTER BEING BOUGHT FROM
LOTUS, JOHNNY HERBERT DROVE
FOR LIGIER, NOW OWNED BY
BENETTON, THE TEAM THAT
DROPPED HERBERT FIVE YEARS
BEFORE . . .

because it was here that Michael and I had joined forces the previous May in order to decide how the safety standards of the circuit could be improved. This was before Jerez had been granted the European Grand Prix – the date originally had been allocated to Argentina but that fell through for various reasons – but we still felt that a few changes were necessary. We sat down with the circuit designers and made our suggestions. They did everything we had asked and the end result was a track which was not only one of the safest but also one which was a pleasure to drive on. Everyone liked it, the only drawback being a shortage of overtaking places. Michael and I had collaborated successfully and now he was slagging me off.

Bernie Ecclestone, the boss of Formula One and a man with an eye for the photo opportunity, suggested that Michael and I should get together on the Saturday to help promote the race and have pictures taken of us shaking hands. This was a clever move as Bernie knew it would make the sports pages simply because it was the oppo-

site of what everyone expected. So, we sat on the pit wall and did our bit. I said to Michael: 'Come on, let's forget all this bullshit and attempts at psychological warfare.' He said: 'Yes, after the championship.' So I said, 'Fine' – and squeezed a little harder when I shook his hand. It was a bit of baloney and razzmatazz which served its purpose and we quickly returned to the more serious business of final qualifying.

It was obvious that the track was going to be quicker because the surface was cleaner than the day before and temperatures were lower due to cloud cover. On Friday, Frentzen had set his time early in the session, which is unusual because the quick times generally come towards the end of qualifying. On this occasion, however, oil had been spilled on the track not long after the start and there was the suspicion that the temperature had gone up as the session went on. It seemed to me that the best thing would be to ignore tradition and go out early in the final session. The problem was, everyone else had the same idea.

MANSELL: THE LION HEART

HMMM . . .

Initially, it was just Hakkinen and me in the queue to leave the pit lane. By the time the track was open, we had been joined by another eight or nine cars. My first attempt at setting a quick time was wasted by traffic as I continually found myself caught behind slower cars. I was unable to improve my time from the previous day and, to make matters worse, other drivers eventually managed to go quicker. In no time at all, I had slipped to seventh place and things were starting to look a little worrying.

I had decided on three runs of two laps each, so I knew I had to re-establish myself with the second set of tyres. This time, I found a clear track and claimed pole position once more. I thought: 'Great! Now let's see what Michael does.' It was a classic qualifying session, in that he went out and beat my time. This left me with the option of either making my final run straight away (the sun was now out and the track would be slower) or waiting until the very end when the cloud might return – but the circuit would be busy. I chose the former.

As I suspected, the track was not as quick but the advantage I was looking for – a clear road – did not materialize. On my last lap, I made a desperate attempt even though I knew the tyres had passed their best. I braked very late for the new chicane and ended up crossing the gravel trap, bringing stones on to the track as I emerged on the far side. That was it. I had to accept the inescapable fact that Michael had drawn first blood by beating me to pole position.

As I got back to the pits, Nigel was making a last attempt to improve on third place. As he came out of the chicane – which is towards the end of the lap – he came on the radio and complained that someone had put rubbish all over the circuit and his lap was ruined. They had to tell him that his team-mate was the culprit.

I was sorry to have inadvertently spoiled his lap. Throughout the weekend, Nigel was amenable and very complimentary; he kept saying that I was doing a great job. The comeback was tough for Nigel since he hadn't done a great deal of driving in a Formula One car and he was still jet-

Nigel had to endure evidence of one or two David Coulthard supporters in the grandstand opposite our pit

lagged following the journey from his final Indycar race in California the previous weekend. On top of this, he had to endure evidence of one or two David Coulthard supporters in the grandstand opposite our pit. One tactless person had gone so far as to prepare a banner which said, 'Nige'! We love ya. But give Coulthard the keys.' Another had a Union Flag which simply said, 'Mansell retire.' I felt that was unkind. It must have been like an arrow through his heart because, in the past, flags bearing Nigel's name had been in abundance and, at places such as Silverstone, represented the support of the entire nation. But Nigel is made of tough stuff.

In any case, he was still in with a shout and, before the race, he suggested that if I was having trouble getting past Schumacher, then I should let him through and he would have a go on my behalf. I thanked him for the gesture, but I didn't really think it was going to happen. No matter how much I respect Nigel, racing drivers are racing drivers and, in the heat of competition, it is naïve to expect any favours. The only certainty was that I would be behind Michael since he was starting from pole, on the clean side of the track and on the right line for the first corner.

As ever, our main preoccupation was trying to guess what his pit stop strategy might be. On paper, two stops would be quicker than three, the only problem being the likelihood of becoming caught behind back-markers before the first stop was due,

something which could cost three seconds a lap and effectively destroy our plan. We decided to go for two stops, but with the option of coming in early should there be a potential problem with slower cars. There seemed less attraction in choosing a three-stop strategy because, if Schumacher was ahead of me (which was reasonable to expect since he was starting from pole) and running to a two-stop plan, I would not be able to overtake on this circuit and enjoy the advantage of running with a light load of fuel. My pace would be dictated by the Benetton even though I had the potential to go much faster. If he was on three stops and I was doing the same, then fine. But we couldn't be sure of that. There was the possibility that Benetton might do something perverse and go against their usual logic by stopping twice instead of the customary three times. Two stops had to be the best option as far as we were concerned.

I received an unexpected bonus when Michael made a bad start. I could see his car creeping forward on the red light and, having been in that situation myself three weeks earlier in Portugal, I knew what was likely to happen. Sure enough, as soon as he touched the brake, the green light came on. I made a perfect start and simply drove past him, taking the lead before the first corner.

I thought: 'Great! We're quids in here. All I have to do is stay ahead.' I was able to manage that quite easily and, when he disappeared into the pits quite early, I was encouraged even more because this suggested he was on a three-stop strategy. This was lap 15, although I didn't know it at

A GREAT START AT JEREZ GAVE ME REAL HOPE FOR THE RACE. THE FINAL RESULT WAS THEREFORE ALL THE MORE DISAPPOINTING

the time because the lap counter on my dashboard display was broken. I fully expected to be out for quite a few laps more before my first stop. Three laps later, the team called me in.

This was much sooner than I had anticipated. I could see one slow car ahead of me but not a string of back-markers which could cause trouble. I wanted to stay out and, in retrospect, I should have got on the radio and said so. Unfortunately, we had organized the pit stop call in such a way that there would be the minimum amount of warning. Usually, there is a count-down on the pit board – three laps to go, two laps, and so on – but, on this occasion, we didn't want to give too much away to the opposition. We relied totally on the radio and, halfway round lap 18, they told me to come in. There was no time to argue about it.

Halfway round lap 18, they told me to come in. There was no time to argue about it

When I returned to the track, Michael was four seconds ahead. His second set of tyres suited the Benetton much better than the first and he really got into his stride. He had overtaken me through having to take less fuel on board and by doing very fast laps entering and leaving the pits. Because of his three-stop strategy, he was running with between 52 and 55 litres on board whereas I had in excess of 70 litres. He began to pull away.

Even so, I continued to feel reasonably confident. Michael had only managed to extend his lead to 14 seconds when he made his second stop. With each visit to the pits taking at least 20 seconds, and him due to make yet another stop, I knew that if I could keep the gap constant, I would

HE'S BACK AGAIN — AND THE GAP
MOVES FROM ONE POINT TO FIVE

still be in good shape. Michael was four seconds behind me when he returned. And I had still some way to go before my second and final stop. Or so I thought.

Two laps later, I was called in. The race had just reached the halfway mark and I was not supposed to stop until around two-thirds distance. I knew something was wrong but, once again, I didn't have time to discuss it. Unbeknown to me, a problem with a seal on the refuelling rig had allowed fuel to seep into the air vent part of the hose. The effect of this was to reduce the level of fuel in the gauge which gave the impression that there was less fuel in the rig than actually went into the car. Of course, nobody realized the full extent of the problem at the time and the impression was that I had received a short measure during my first fuel stop. Naturally, they were worried that I might run out of fuel.

The effect of all of this was that I received something like 100 litres during that final stop in order to see me through to the end of the race. And, of course, nobody realized that there was a considerable amount of fuel already in the tank. So, I set off with around 120 litres on board. By comparison, Michael had just left the pits a few laps before with no more than 55 litres in his tank. In other words, I had over twice the amount of fuel – with 33 laps still to go. And, of course, I had to go all that way on one set of tyres which were about to receive a lot of abuse because of the heavy fuel load. It was like having a passenger plus a full load of luggage in the car. My race was over from that point on. There was no way I could either stay with Michael or get

I had gone from the feeling that I had a good chance of winning to one of being well and truly stuffed

the optimum from the car. Plus, with such a heavy car, it was extremely difficult to get past back-markers. Having looked so good in the early stages, my race had fallen apart.

I couldn't necessarily blame the team because they did what they could under the circumstances. But that did not alter the feeling of total helplessness. When the race finished, I knew we had been completely thrashed. It had not even been a close run thing, something which would keep Schumacher and Benetton on their toes. Added to which, Nigel had not really figured very much before spinning off on lap 48. It was a massive victory for Benetton and it made me extremely angry. In the space of a few laps, I had gone from the feeling that I had a good chance of winning to one of being well and truly stuffed.

It had been a disaster – but not a total disaster. The championship gap had gone from one point to five points with two races to go. This result had been extremely painful but, if nothing else, it was to spur us on. Despite the fact that we had now been written off in certain quarters, those first 14 laps proved that we could beat the opposition. We were not as bad – and Benetton were not as strong – as the final result suggested.

CHAPTER TWELVE
THE FINAL SHOWDOWN
THE JAPANESE AND AUSTRALIAN GRANDS PRIX

The final two races of the season in Japan and Australia were obviously going to be of huge importance but you wouldn't have thought so, judging by the way we started our preparations. We went to Portugal for a couple of days and it was unquestionably the worst test session of the year.

I had a big accident, then it rained, we had an engine failure and, overall, the car wasn't very quick. To say we left Estoril with our tails between our legs would hardly be an exaggeration.

I wasn't hurt as such by the accident but I was pretty badly shaken. I didn't bang my head or anything like that but when you hit the barrier at around 120 m.p.h., it gives the body a bit of a jolt, to say the least. In actual fact, I think I had mild concussion because I was feeling shaky for some time afterwards and I had difficulty standing up. A detailed medical check-up soon revealed nothing more than delayed shock.

The accident had been the result of a straightforward but potentially lethal sequence of events. It had been raining but the track itself was dry. However, the joints between the kerbs edging the track still contained water and, when I put a rear wheel on the kerb, water was flicked on the tyre.

Suddenly, from having maximum grip at the exit of this very quick corner, I had

IT'S GOOD TO TALK — BUT
NOT HERE. MICHAEL SCHUMACHER
ATTEMPTS TO MAKE A PRIVATE
CALL BEFORE AN APPRECIATIVE
AUDIENCE AT THE
BENETTON OFFICE

none at all. The car was sideways and into the barrier in less time than it has taken you to read this sentence. I had arrived in Estoril fired up and determined to go quickly but the accident was a stark reminder that a racing car can bite back if you don't give it the respect it deserves.

It was confirmation that absolutely nothing can be overlooked. Part of my plan for the final two races was to fly out a week early but to go to Hong Kong to begin the recovery from jet lag rather than hanging around in Japan.

When I arrived there on the Thursday, I was immediately engulfed by the car-crazy fans. Going from A to B was a major problem. Signing autographs and having your picture taken incessantly can be hard to bear at the best of times but it becomes very wearing on top of jet lag, particularly at such a critical stage in the season. By the end of practice on the first day, Friday, I have to admit that the pressure was beginning to tell.

During my first runs in the morning I encountered a lot of traffic and therefore could not set a competitive time. This provoked Patrick Head into interrupting a conversation over the radio between myself and David Brown in the garage trying to sort out some problems in an attempt to get things moving.

Patrick seemed to be losing his patience and was making comments to the effect that I had better get a move on because, at the moment, I wasn't competitive, which was the kind of obvious statement I felt didn't need saying and just cost time that could have been better spent trying to discuss with David ways to improve the car. But this frustration was symptomatic of the desire we all felt to win this race.

'You've got a lot to learn before you become a driver like Nigel'

To add to my worries, the car did not feel particularly good. In order to do a reasonable time, I really had to go to the limit, and still 'Schuey' was four-tenths quicker. I was second fastest – reasonable enough, you might think – but Michael had provisional pole and he had done his time with apparent ease. I hadn't slept well the previous evening and, all told, I was pretty grumpy.

After qualifying, I was trying to explain my general dissatisfaction with the car to Patrick and Frank and, once again, I felt I was making observations which were not being taken seriously because, when Nigel Mansell said more or less the same thing, his comments seemed to make a greater impression on Patrick than I felt mine had.

My remarks on this provoked Patrick into explaining to me why he thought this was and it went something along the lines of: 'You've got a lot to learn before you become a driver like Nigel' – along with other comments which would be unfair to print but which I found really negative and which took me aback. All I could reply was, 'Thanks for being so open. At least now I know where I stand.' After this frank exchange, I was scheduled to meet with the British press, as per normal, but because I was fuming I could only manage to get out, 'There is nothing to say,' as I pushed past them.

The situation now was that the car was going to be difficult to drive for 53 laps around Suzuka and I felt pretty demoralized by Patrick's comments. Not the ideal platform from which to launch an attack on the over-confident German. Here I was, on the eve of the final qualifying for the most important race of the season so far, feeling as though the team bosses were showing less than total confidence in my ability. If I needed moral support, it seemed I would have to look elsewhere. That night I spent a considerable time on the phone to my wife Georgie because I was seriously considering the best alternative route for my career. Things are never what they seem from the outside.

Because of the difficulty of access imposed by the large numbers of fans, the drivers were taken back and forth to the circuit by helicopter, a flight lasting just a couple of minutes but the only way to make the 500-yard journey without being mobbed. On Friday morning, the trip had been an impressive experience due to clear blue skies. On Saturday, it was like going to a different place, as grey mist cloaked the huge funfair outside the track.

The good news was that we had the car working much better. Nigel was on excellent form and he set the fastest time in the morning session. I was having trouble achieving the same result as Nigel on a certain part of the circuit. Again, this was very frustrating but, thanks to Nigel's efforts, I at least knew that the car could do it. This is a good example of how two drivers can push each other to their mutual benefit. I finally managed to sort myself out although a potentially quick lap towards the end of the session was spoiled by slower cars. So, ultimately I was not quickest, which served to rev me up even more.

Ultimately I was not quickest, which served to rev me up even more

All that became irrelevant during the break before the final qualifying. Rain began to fall and, unbeknown to everyone, the track would never be dry again for the rest of the weekend. The only good thing to be said was that the grid was now set, based on times from Friday, and I would be starting from the front row.

I felt very tired after qualifying. The temptation was to go to bed at about 4 p.m. but I made myself stay awake until later in the evening. There was no point in going to sleep early because it would simply have meant waking up at about 1 a.m., raring to go.

I finally enjoyed a decent night's sleep on Saturday and that relieved some of the pressure. Michael may have been on pole but I felt that the fight was by no means over. The track was damp during the warm-up on race morning and we hoped it might be dry for the race. As the day wore on, however, it became really dark and gloomy. Then the rain set in.

We had been criticized for poor strategy at Jerez but the team would dispute that because of the problems we had with the refuelling rig. But the fact was, we had to get it absolutely right this time. To make the right decision, there were all sorts of problems to consider, such as the lap being split almost exactly in half, one section of the track being very twisty and the other being not quite so bad. If the entire track is twisty, it is better to stop more often for tyres and fuel because a lighter car is better suited to this sort of circuit layout. But with the track being split, it is much more difficult to make that decision.

On the other hand, if the race is run in the rain, then everything is different again because it is possible to do many more laps on rain tyres (as opposed to slicks) without losing time in pit stops simply because the wear-rate of the wet tyres is not so critical. And, because of the visibility problems in the spray, I would prefer not to stop

THE FINAL SHOWDOWN

257

at all. Losing a place in the field becomes a major problem because of difficulties created by trying to fight back through the traffic.

It was impossible to predict anything and yet I was facing a most crucial race from my point of view. The only way to look at it was to say that I wanted to be World Champion. That being the case, I had to win at Suzuka. If I did that and Michael finished second, the gap between us would be one point. If those positions were reversed, the gap would be nine points – and that was no use whatsoever. I simply had to win and this was an enormous personal challenge. I was going to have to drive like I had never driven before; hang the risk.

The race was going to last close to two hours; two hours of total concentration and maximum pressure

Being wet added another degree of difficulty. The chances of falling off the track are far greater than they are in the dry. Corners which are taken flat out with no trouble at all on a dry surface suddenly become very tricky curves in the wet. The very poor visibility requires enormous concentration – even while driving down the straight – and, under these conditions, the race was going to last close to two hours; two hours of total concentration and maximum pressure.

All this was going through my mind as I sat on the grid. I was facing a watershed. I was either going to come out of this triumphant or – the alternative was not worth contemplating. In some ways, it would be a relief finally to get going and answer the question. Now it was down to me.

Nigel was right behind me, sharing the second row with Heinz-Harald Frentzen in the Sauber-Mercedes. So I had two very pumped drivers, keen to get a good result, sitting on my tail and threatening to make things even more difficult than they already were. But I had spoken to Nigel before the race and he said that, while he was out to do the best he could for himself, he was also there to help me win the championship. I knew he was sincere in that. I also knew he was very experienced and would not do anything silly, whereas Frentzen had nothing to lose and everything to gain. But, most importantly, I was just thinking of Michael and how he was going to handle all this.

When the lights changed, we both made pretty appalling starts. It was almost impossible to get off the line. The track was very slippery and we both got a lot of wheelspin. Indeed, I was surprised that we were not overtaken. It seems like a lifetime when you are sitting there and the car is just not going forward. It is a relief to finally get traction and speed away from the line.

Michael slewed across in front of me to try to protect the line into the first corner to make sure I didn't actually come down the inside. It was difficult to say whether it was an attempt to push me out of the way or an attempt to control his car because we were both snaking widely, struggling to find grip. I'd give him the benefit of the doubt and any uncharitable thoughts were soon dispelled by the reception waiting for us at the first corner at the bottom of the hill.

We were greeted by the most amazing sight I have ever witnessed on the first lap of a race

We were greeted by the most amazing sight I have ever witnessed on the first lap of a race. Surrounding the first corner is a two-storey grandstand containing about 20,000 spectators and it was glittering with many bright white flashes from all the cameras frantically capturing the moment. Because of the dull conditions, the effect was truly stunning and all this time I'm sliding along behind Michael in his spray.

It seemed to me that Michael was being pretty cautious on the first lap but even so, he very nearly went off. Someone had dropped oil during the parade lap and the effect of the oil mixing with water created a rainbow effect on the track surface. He hit it first and missed the apex of the corner. The next thing, he was sideways, heading towards the gravel.

I was saying, 'Go on, Michael! Go on! Don't hang on to it!' I was definitely wishing him to go off; I couldn't help it.

There were a few more corners where there was oil and he very nearly went off again. He was on the limit and struggling to stay ahead but, of course, I was receiving adequate warning about the oil, thanks to his antics. Unfortunately Frentzen behind me ended up taking a trip into the sand trap.

After a couple of laps, the heavens opened: there was a torrential downpour. I got on the radio and said, 'They've got to stop this; it's ridiculous. It's impossible to even drive down the straight.' I heard David Brown's reassuring voice saying: 'Hang on, you're doing fine. They're bringing the safety car out.'

But I was already going at half speed and the car was aquaplaning; simply water-skiing, floating along the top of the water. It could go anywhere; you simply had no idea what it was going to do next. It was like sliding on a tray on an ice rink.

Seeing the safety car was a relief although two or three cars went off on the straight, one of them smashing into the concrete wall right by the Williams pit. Michael, too, had to fall in behind the safety car but I discovered later that he had been

THE SAFETY CAR LEADS THE FIELD

THROUGH THE GLOOM

on the radio saying that he couldn't keep up with it! It took several laps to clear the wreckage, and, this time, allowed the water to disperse.

Throughout the time I was on the radio, trying to find out what was happening next. Michael, meanwhile, was speeding up and slowing down, slamming on his brakes on the straight, trying to catch me out because, of course, the rules say that you are not supposed to overtake on these occasions – as Michael and Benetton knew only too well. I didn't fall for it.

The most important thing was to maintain concentration and remain fired up. When the safety car finally pulled off, Michael made a fantastic job of the re-start. He timed it very well and managed to pull away.

Three laps later, they stopped the race. By this stage, there had been a couple of big accidents and, I must say, I was not surprised because the conditions were appalling. It seems it happens all too often when it's really wet. Sometimes, the organizers do not appreciate how difficult it is to drive under these circumstances but we were very lucky that no one was seriously hurt. In actual fact, a marshal's leg was broken when Martin Brundle spun off at the scene of a previous accident where officials were trying to remove an abandoned car.

It was a relief to see the red flag and this meant that the race would now be in two parts, the results being decided on aggregate times from the two. In other words, Michael had been 6.8 seconds ahead of me and he would carry that through the second part even if we were level-pegging on the track.

This delay was another problem to overcome. Normally, when waiting on the grid during the final half hour before the start, I would get out of the car. But this time I hadn't done that. And I didn't get out during this period while the race was stopped because I didn't want to get my driving boots wet and, in any case, there would not be that much time. So, I waited in the car even though I was actually sitting on a pool of water.

When following the safety car during the deluge, the cockpit had just filled with water. There was so much water being flicked up by the tyres and coming from the car in front, it was, without exaggeration, like someone spraying you with a hose. You have to keep your visor open on these occasions to keep the air flow coming through and stopping everything from fogging up. Unfortunately this also allows the rain to come inside the helmet. Wet weather racing is a whole different experience.

I was right with Michael as he suddenly accelerated. I was ready for him this time

Once we were ready to start again, fifteen minutes later, we set off behind the safety car – which I thought was a good idea – rather than attempting a potentially dangerous standing start. We did two laps like that and, once again, Michael seemed to be trying to catch me out by suddenly braking. I very nearly went into the back of him at one point. The idea was to let the pace car get ahead so that we would be up to racing speed at the point, just as it pulled off. I was determined not to be left behind this time and, as we crawled along, I closed right up on Michael and started to weave around behind him. I wanted to keep him looking in his mirrors and cause a distraction just at the point where he should have been working out how and when to make a sudden break. It must have worked because I was right with him as he suddenly accelerated. I was ready for him this time.

So, we were off again – and to my surprise, he dived into the pits after five laps. I was not due to stop for another seven laps and, during this time, I made the most of the clear road and took the lead. Michael returned to the track, heavy with fuel and in among the top six runners. He had fallen into the strategy trap he had managed to avoid in earlier races.

When my turn came to make my one and only stop, the mechanics could not remove my right-rear tyre, although I was not aware of the difficulty. Had we been running on slick tyres, of course, this would have been a big problem because the tyre would probably not have taken another stint. But, because we were on wet tyres, it was not so critical, so I was sent on my way with the original right-rear tyre still in place.

I was in the lead, both on the road and on corrected time, and the team were keeping me informed of the gap, which was coming down because, although I did not know it, Michael was running with less fuel on board. There was a massive television screen for the benefit of the spectators of the chicane and occasionally I could get a glimpse of Michael on the screen. I could see where he was relative to me on the track but, of course, the strange thing was that this bore no relation to the actual race position since he still had that 6.8 seconds to his advantage.

I pushed like mad to make sure he did not eat away at my lead. The difficulty was that he could take the lead without actually having to overtake me on the road, which was making it easier for him because, if we had been racing under normal circumstances, it would have been one thing for him to catch me and quite another for him physically to overtake. Even if he was quicker than me, I could have held him up. But this was not a good situation from my point of view because, thanks to the race being in two parts, the aggregate times meant he could take the lead even though he was still behind me on the road. Sometimes, you have to be on the ball to follow a Grand Prix.

Michael chopped away at the gap and took the lead – and there was nothing I could do. I was pushing as hard as I could and he was continuing to extend the gap. Then he made my day by pulling into the pits! This explained a lot because, obviously, he had next to no fuel on board whereas I had enough to see me through the final 10 laps. My immediate reaction was to be careful and not extend myself the way I had been. The track was still treacherous and I did a slow lap. I quickly realized that I had lost too much to Michael. I had to press on since this was the only way to guarantee my lead now that Michael was back on the track with the benefit of a fresh set of tyres. I knew he was going to be quick.

He was taking a couple of seconds a lap off me and my lead started to come down from 14 seconds, to 11, then 9 seconds. With seven laps to go, I knew it was going to be close. All the time, of course, I was being told the gap by radio. Going into

the final lap, Michael was 2.4 seconds behind. This was going to be the nail-biter of all time. I also knew this was now or never. If I wanted to win the championship, I was going to have to drive like never before. If he beat me, the gap between us at the end of the race would be nine points. If I won the race, it would be a single point. For the first time ever, I actually experienced the emotion of the moment while in the car. One half of my brain saying, 'Come on, come on! You can do it!' And the other half was cracking up! But I knew I had to go for it.

TEMPORARY HOLD-UP. THE MASKED AND GOGGLED WILLIAMS CREW PREPARE TO POUNCE ON MY CAR DURING OUR ONE AND ONLY PIT STOP

THE FINAL SHOWDOWN

YEEESS! I HAD TO BEAT
SCHUMACHER IN JAPAN AND
THAT'S EXACTLY WHAT I DID.
BUT IT WASN'T EASY . . .

Coming out of the last chicane, I could not get the power on quickly enough. If I lost the race by a couple of thousandths of a second, I would be forever thinking that maybe I could have come out of the last corner just a tiny bit quicker and that would have won the race. I was doing everything I possibly could and, in actual fact, I went a second quicker than I had done before and extended my lead. It was the lap of my life, the big one in every sense.

The trouble was, I had to wait until Michael crossed the line before knowing whether or not I had done enough. I had finished first but I didn't know if I had won. Nobody did. As soon as Michael took the flag, the computer flashed up the gap: 3.3 seconds. The championship was down to one point.

There was a scramble to give me the news on the radio, several people shouting at once with the result so that I couldn't understand a thing they were saying. Eventually I heard the magic words 'P1'. I had won and I let out a big 'Yahoo!'

I spent the slowing down lap coming back to reality, trying to believe that I had done it, that it was all over.

Quite apart from all that, it had been a fantastic race and I had been able to drive the way I know I can if I have to. I'd had the opportunity to show what I can do. When I reached parc ferme, I switched off the engine and just sat in the car for a second or two. I had been in the cockpit for close to three hours and I was trying to collect myself after all that mental and physical effort.

In any case, even though no one is allowed into parc ferme – the cars need to be examined by the scrutineers before anyone else can touch them – most of the team was pressed against the barrier and I could see they were very, very happy. I just wanted to savour that for a moment or two.

Michael came over and shook my hand and then gave me a playful slap on the helmet. But, deep down, he knew how hard he had driven and yet he had lost. I think it was a bit of a shock since he had been pretty confident all weekend. On top of that, he had been beaten by someone he had referred to as a second-rate driver. I was interested to know how he would cope with that!

We had won through a combination of the right tactics, my driving – and a little bit of luck. And there was a poignancy to all this since it had happened in Japan, a place which holds Ayrton Senna in very high esteem. Ayrton won all three of his championships in Japan. Two hours before the race a helicopter, painted in the vivid colours of Ayrton's helmet, delivered his sister, Viviane, and his cousin, Fabio Machado, to the grid where they took part in a moving ceremony in Ayrton's memory. Considering the significance of being in Suzuka and the fact that Ayrton had played such an important part during our all-too-brief association, I felt it appropriate to dedicate my win to his family, in his memory. I would very much like to think that my race at Suzuka came close to the sort of performance of which he would have been proud.

An hour or so after the race, a journalist asked about my contract and I made some comments to the effect that negotiations were still going on with Frank concerning my retainer for 1995. I didn't think much more about it after that, but the subject was to return with a vengeance before the week was out.

I was supposed to leave Osaka for Australia that night but, unfortunately, Jon Nicholson's bags – with passport, business material and pictures for this book – got loaded into a taxi and taken to Nagoya. We couldn't leave until they were recovered later on Monday, which meant we had to spend the day waiting at Suzuka.

I had arranged to go to my old hero Barry Sheene's house and, the moment we arrived in Brisbane, he had a helicopter waiting to whisk us down to Surfers' Paradise. The weather was terrific. I flew the helicopter down the coast and then Barry took us for a mile or two at about 100 feet above the beach. It was a most exhilarating way to arrive.

As soon as we reached his house, Barry got out his toys – a wet bike and water-skiing kit – and we just played around in the waterway at the back of his house. The wet bike was a bit of a beast and I felt extremely precarious but Barry said, 'Right, you're going to tow me; I'm going water-skiing.' I had only ridden this wet bike once about ten minutes earlier. I managed to pull him up and took him for a tow – which I think was one of the main reasons why he had invited us down there! The most alarming thing was when he fell off and broke his wrist. He didn't realize it at the time but when it began to hurt later that night, he had to go to hospital. I had also fallen off once or twice and I was only thankful the injury wasn't mine, but at least Barry's getting used to breaking bones by now.

It was all too short a stay and I had to leave the next day for Adelaide. When

FED UP — OR WHAT? MICHAEL SCHUMACHER'S EXPRESSION SAYS IT ALL AS HE TAKES SECOND PLACE ON THE ROSTRUM

PUTTING THE BOOT IN.
SQUEEZING MY SIZE ELEVENS
INTO THE COCKPIT OF THE
WILLIAMS IS NOT THE WORK OF
A MOMENT

I arrived, a press conference had been set up at the airport. On the way, I had been thinking further about the contract situation.

After Suzuka, I again had the distinct impression that the support from Frank and Patrick was not whole-hearted. Whether or not my views were misplaced, that was how I felt. I was being messed around in my discussions for the next year and, with my performance at Suzuka, I showed that I was capable of taking the pressure and driving at the very top level of Formula One.

I thought it would be appropriate, if asked any questions about the contract negotiations, that I should let people know that throughout the period since Frank had taken up the option on my contract, I had been struggling to get a clear indication of how much I was valued by the team. I felt it was entirely wrong that I had been put under this stress when I was supposed to be fighting for the championship, particularly as they knew that I was their only hope of regaining the title. I couldn't understand why my mind hadn't been put at rest. I wanted it to be known that I was doing what I was doing under this cloud.

At the press conference, I made a few pointed remarks and, I must say, I said too much and in the wrong way. I didn't get my point across very well. There was lot of misunderstanding and it was pounced upon. I can't blame the press because I gave them the material in the first place. It seemed to take on its own momentum. Before I knew it, I had created a major controversy.

And yet, I felt I had got the subject out in the open. It was a rather unhappy way to arrive in Adelaide, especially after what had happened at Suzuka. However, I felt I had nothing to lose because, in some ways, my situation still wasn't clear. Nonetheless, I had some explaining to do when I arrived at the circuit. Once you have opened a can of worms like that, it is not very easy to put the lid back on.

On the one hand, I wanted to stand by what I had said but, on the other, I didn't want it to overwhelm the entire meeting. So I had some discussions with Frank and Patrick and, obviously, Frank said he was pretty unhappy. I said I was pretty unhappy too that this should be happening. They were both worried that it was going to distract me at such a crucial time.

I then held a press conference at the circuit and tried to back-pedal a little bit by drawing attention to the fact that this was an exciting finale to the championship. But my efforts at directing media attention away from questions about the contract were hardly successful because I had started the ball rolling in the first place. It was a very uncomfortable occasion. But you live and learn. This was new territory for me and I realized I have a lot to learn about politics and negotiation strategies in Formula One.

Finance is a very relevant part of the whole job. There is a great deal of money in Formula One and you have to fight for your share if you believe you deserve it. No one will offer more money just because you're a nice chap. That much is clear. When I started to drive for Frank, he was giving me the opportunity of a lifetime. I knew the contract was pretty paltry but I was given an ultimatum; either sign the contract or you don't get the drive. I had no negotiating power at all. I signed the contract and had to live with the consequences.

But I took the view that I would show what I am worth, sense would prevail and we could renegotiate. Even though it is not the done thing to go back on what had been agreed in the beginning, I still could not see the reason for having a driver who was dissatisfied within the team. That would not be the best way to motivate me. Frank and Patrick's view seemed to me to be that they could make the driver hungry by having him always needing to prove that he is worth more, therefore he drives faster.

Obviously, I take a different view. I feel that to get the best out of a driver you have to make him feel good; you have to make him feel that the people close to him believe in him and his capacity to do the job. And this is expressed at least partly by how much they are prepared to pay for his driving services. In Formula One terms, in the context of the whole budget and the investment by Rothmans and Renault, the amount I was getting, I felt, was disproportionate to the responsibility. Ultimately, the hopes of Renault Sport in Paris, Rothmans and more than 200 people at Williams lay

'TAKE IT FROM ME.'
HAVING BEEN INVOLVED IN
MANY A CHAMPIONSHIP SHOOT-
OUT, NIGEL MANSELL GIVES
ADVICE AND ENCOURAGEMENT.
NIGEL PROVIDED THE TEAM
WITH THE CONSOLATION OF
VICTORY IN ADELAIDE

on my performances. Okay, they were not going to go under if I didn't get results but, by the same token, every result is crucial and a matter of pride to companies with such high standards.

I knew of drivers in Formula One who were earning a lot more than I was and yet they had not won a single race. I had won nine grands prix – as many as Gerhard Berger – and it was only my second season. Like it or not, money is a motivating factor to a professional racing driver. There are a lot of downsides of course. I would never complain about the job I have got but it is very time-consuming, it is very dangerous and you don't honestly know how long your career is going to last. It is important that,

I knew of drivers in Formula One who were earning a lot more than I was and yet they had not won a single race

when you are at your peak, you are earning the appropriate amount of money. That's the way I felt about it. But this didn't get around the fact that I had signed a contract! That was the bottom line.

Whatever the rights and wrongs of the situation, it was an awkward start to the weekend. But, when I got into the car on Friday, I felt I had unburdened myself in much the same way that I had attacked the press at Silverstone. I felt free of an extra worry because as I saw it I was already on a sticky wicket and I had nothing to lose by saying what I did. I was in the right frame of mind to drive and I was quickest in the first practice session. I felt good and the car felt great.

In qualifying, however, things did not go well at all. The first run wasn't quick, the car did not feel right – I had a lot of understeer – and the session really was a bit of a struggle. I was making a lot of mistakes because I couldn't get the car to do what I wanted it to do.

The good news was that Nigel was quickest. And, into the bargain, Michael had the biggest accident he has had for quite some time. It was clear that he was trying hard. I was trying my best not to be despondent, even though I was only third quickest.

The following morning, I managed just four laps before I spun off. We had made some revised parts for the car but we only had a limited number. The worry was that the damage might be severe enough to force us to go back to a standard specification, but fortunately, once the car was returned to the garage, we found such a retrograde step would not be necessary. When it rained for final qualifying, the grid positions were set based on Friday's times; Nigel on pole, Michael second fastest with me third, on the inside of the second row.

The main thing was that I was close to Michael and, with Nigel on the front

UNDETERRED BY BACKGROUND
INTERFERENCE FROM THE
RACE TRACK, ALTERNATIVE
ENTERTAINMENT GIVES FULL
NOISE FROM BEHIND THE
GRANDSTAND

row, it meant Williams could think about tactics and work as a team towards winning the Constructors' Championship (which we led by five points from Benetton) and the one I was mainly interested in, the Drivers' Championship.

Each evening I had been trying to get away from the pressure and I had supper at the same Italian restaurant every night. I followed a routine in order to get myself as relaxed as I could. I did the same thing on the night before the race. I ate with friends, one of whom, Peter Boutwood, had been so concerned after reading the press reports in Britain that he had jumped on a plane on Thursday and arrived in Adelaide on Saturday morning. He was only going to be there for three days, but it was good to see him. Also, my solicitor, Michael Breen, came out for a short stay because we felt it could be important to have him present in Adelaide, after my comments following Suzuka. Imagine going to Australia for just three days!

Georgie stayed in England because we thought it was right for one parent to stay at home. I didn't want the children coming all the way to Australia; it is a very long trip and they like to maintain their routine as much as anyone else. Besides, I wanted to keep my head clear as much as possible for the job which had to be done the next day.

I managed to sleep very well on Saturday night. I felt relaxed. In fact, the only thing which worried me was the fact that I was too relaxed. It is always a concern for

ALL EARS. IAN HARRISON
CONCENTRATES HARD BY THE
PIT WALL DURING HIS FINAL STINT
AS F1 TEAM MANAGER BEFORE
SWITCHING TO THE WILLIAMS
TOURING CAR TEAM FOR 1995

any competitor to get the right amount of adrenalin flowing. If you have too much, you just wear yourself out before the start of a race; you can't sleep, you can't relax, you can't think. But if you fail to get enough adrenalin, you don't extract enough performance out of yourself. It is an art knowing your own condition and mental state.

Going into the half-hour warm-up on race morning, the car was not that quick. But I did the whole session on an old set of tyres. A lot of people had used the session to scrub in a new set of tyres which they would use for the race; they hadn't had a chance to do that because of the wet weather. You can't go into a race on a brand new set of tyres; you have to have a little bit of running on them so that they are not shiny and they have had a chance to cure by going through one heat cycle.

My car felt good even though I was not that fast. It was a bit of a worry but, even so, the abiding impression was that I liked what the car was doing; I liked the way it put the power down, it had good traction, it was quite good on the brakes. I could actually manage the car quite well. I could get it turned into a corner easily and get back on the power quickly. That stuck with me, so I didn't change the car for the race; I was happy with the way things were.

The only thing to think about was pit stop tactics. Given that we had come in for a lot of comment over our pit stops in the past — when we made two and Benetton won with three — we knew that this would be critical from many points of view, not least being that we had reached the final round of the championship. We wanted to do the right thing but we did not want to be pushed into a certain tactic because we had been criticized for doing the opposite in the past. Using a lot of calculations, we predicted that the race would be roughly the same whether we made two or three stops. We chose to make three stops and our feeling was that Michael would do the same.

With Nigel, however, we thought it would be better to go for two stops because he was ahead on the grid. Even if he was slow, it would not matter because he would be in front and, with our horsepower advantage, he would be able to stay

ahead of Michael on the straight. He might even slow him down and allow me to stay close to the Benetton.

I was confident that we had done everything right. We had worked it all out and there was nothing niggling in the back of my mind that I wasn't happy about. I liked the car and I liked the strategy.

I managed to spend about twenty minutes lying on the floor, in a quiet spot of the garage, almost asleep, in order to calm myself before the start of the race. And yet I was still worried about being too relaxed. Sometimes you can go the other way and reach the point where you gnaw things over and you can't write your own name because your hand is shaking. That hasn't happened to me often. But for this race, I felt really calm and I was worried that I would not get the adrenalin flowing. Josef gave me his last-minute massage and reflexology. He touches pressure points in order to stimulate whatever it is he is trying to stimulate. All I know is that it really hurts. Patrick came in at the very moment Josef was pulling my earlobes so hard I thought he would rip them off! He gave us a very strange look but I was prepared to go through all this if it would help. I did worry, however, that Josef's adrenalin was flowing stronger than even he realized.

My feeling was that everything counted. I been given trinkets and bits and pieces by people for luck but I didn't take any of them with me to the car because I knew I had everything I needed within myself. But I respected the intent with which they were given. I had received many faxes and, each time I returned to my room, the floor was littered with good luck messages shoved under the door. I had all the support I could possibly wish for.

There was also a good amount of encouragement from within the paddock. I'm sure it was the same for Michael but anyone in my position would feed off that to make themselves stronger and more confident. Even Patrick said, 'Look, Damon, whatever happens in this race, I think you've done a bloody good job this season.' Patrick is not known for being free with his compliments but I knew he meant what he said. We had what amounted to a reconciliation and that was good because it added to the feeling of well-being before the battle. Nigel was also very supportive, saying that I had done a terrific job all season and he was going to help me in any way he could. The general mood was that we had done everything we possibly could. Now we were going to find out whether or not we deserved the championship. It was a feeling of being ready for whatever lay ahead – and that was the perfect way to go into the race. I wasn't nervous or anxious. I was simply very well prepared.

Coming on to the grid, I felt less tense than I had done in other, much less significant races

Once I was strapped into the car, the adrenalin did start to flow. I timed it really well and I knew then that my focus was sharp. Coming on to the grid, I felt less tense than I had done in other, much less significant races.

When the lights changed, I made a good start. But so did Michael, on my right. Nigel, who was ahead of us, got too much wheelspin. During my planning, I had a mental picture of making a better start than Michael and Nigel and then going through to the right to take the racing line into the first corner, knowing that Nigel would not move across on me. But it didn't happen that way and I had to go to the left, which was dusty and slippery. Michael was on the correct line, which meant he could take the correct line into the fast sweep of the first corner. I had to back off and let him go through because, obviously, I didn't want to jeopardize anything at that point, but it was a close thing.

I knew I was in front of Nigel but, really, the worst possible thing had happened because Michael was in the lead. I did not want him to have a clear track because he simply flies and, on this occasion, he was bound to drive like he had never driven before. Sure enough, he started to pull away, but only for a lap and a half. I then found I could stay with him. I was pushing, not beyond my limit, but to the limit of the equipment. The gap started to reduce.

I looked in my mirror: Nigel wasn't anywhere to be seen. Neither was Hakkinen, who had been alongside me on the second row of the grid, although I had it on good authority that he would not cause me any problems at the start, so it was just me and Michael.

After about 15 laps, we caught the first of the back-markers. Occasionally Michael went wide and he did not seem as committed as usual when lapping the slower cars. He appeared a little bit uncertain about taking a chance.

Once, going down the back straight, I made the most of a good aerodynamic tow from the Benetton as we reached 180 m.p.h.. Then it was hard on the brakes as

LET BATTLE COMMENCE.
NIGEL MOVES TO HIS RIGHT,
BUT MICHAEL IS ALREADY ON HIS
WAY THROUGH. I HAVE NO
ALTERNATIVE BUT TO TAKE TO
THE DIRTY SIDE OF THE TRACK
ON MY LEFT

we scrambled down to 60 m.p.h. for the next corner. We had come upon a back-marker. Michael went down the inside and I was right behind him, getting closer and closer. My front brakes were locking up – and I was almost into the back of his car. I tried to make sure that, if I hit him, I didn't do it with my front wings. I was attempting not to hit him at all, but if I couldn't avoid it, the best thing would be to hit his tyre with the middle of my front nose-cone, so as not to break my wings. But, when your brakes are locked, it is impossible to steer. It was a very close moment. We got round the corner somehow but the experience was typical of my commitment and desire to stay with him and also not to allow a back-marker to get between us.

When it was time for the first pit stop, we both went in at exactly the same moment. The most excruciating thing of all was going down the pit lane with one finger on the speed limit control in order to prevent the car from exceeding the 80 k.p.h. pit lane safety speed. Up until that point, we had been racing furiously. The next moment, we were pootling down the pit road a few car lengths apart at exactly the same speed and yet I knew that if I could only take my finger off the button I would catch him in no time at all. Both our garages were at the far end of the pit lane and it seemed to take forever to get there.

Michael dived into his pit and I overtook him on my way to the Williams area. For that brief period, I was ahead on the road although the pit stop itself seemed to take an eternity. It was high anxiety because the slightest fumble could have cost a vital second or two. The pit work was perfect and just as I was thinking we might snatch the lead – wham! – Michael shot past the second I received the signal to go.

We were off again, picking up as before, although the gap was slightly bigger. At one point he got a clear track and set a series of very quick laps. He was really pushing and I went over a kerb at the exit of one corner and then locked my brakes going into another. I lost further time when a back-marker got between us. I had to force myself to calm down and concentrate totally on driving smoothly. I did that, and the gap began to close.

Michael was so far to the left that I thought there was no way he could change direction quickly enough to take the line for the corner

I knew it would be danger time once he started to disappear around corners before I had even reached them. I could not afford to let him get out of my sight because then he could relax for a little, while, at the same time, I would be going flat out trying to catch him. This was the big one and I could do nothing less.

He must have been well and truly on the limit on lap 36. I came into the first left-hander in a sequence of corners and, as I came through, I saw Michael scrabbling across the grass, trying to get back on the track. Straight away, I knew that this was an absolutely crucial moment. The pressure was paying off. It seemed to me that he had lost control momentarily, but I knew he would soon be back on the road and away again. In the past, I had seen him have bad moments from which he was able to recover very quickly. I did not presume that his car was damaged but I did think that he might have lost time.

Since he was slow getting out of the corner, I attempted to go to his left because it looked as if he was going to protect the line on the right going into the next right-hand bend. But he came all the way across the track to the left. I got on the brakes and nearly hit him. Then I came off the brakes and darted right. I gave the car a squirt of throttle. He was so far to the left that I thought there was no way he could change direction quickly enough to take the line for the corner.

Thinking this could be my only chance to overtake, I darted down the inside. I had to go for it. As I got closer to the apex of the right-hander, he started to come across. Very acutely. It was obvious that he was not going to take a wide line. I didn't know whether his steering was damaged, but the Benetton was going to protect the inside line with no regard for the fact that I was there. And I was pretty sure he knew exactly where I was. I went over the kerb on the right to give him more room. But we touched.

The first impact came when my left front wheel hit his side-pod. Then his right rear wheel went over my left front and that flipped the Benetton into the air. It looked to me as if he was going to go right over. I was thinking, 'Jesus – I hope he's going to be all right.' I saw him land the right way up and go nose first into a tyre wall, so it was obvious that he would be okay.

Then I noticed that my suspension was damaged. I couldn't believe it. I had trouble turning the wheel and I realized pretty quickly that was probably the end of it because the job of changing the front suspension would take fifteen to twenty minutes. Even so, I struggled back to the pits. There were a few attempts to do something but it was hopeless. It was with great difficulty that everyone had to accept that the championship was over.

I got out of the car and walked into the garage. I didn't feel angry or choked or demoralized because everyone was coming up and saying, 'What a great drive. You really gave him a run for his money. The race was terrific up to that point. You couldn't have done anything else.' But there was very little consolation in the bald fact that I had not won.

The race was still going on and Nigel was fighting for the lead. Williams at least knew they had won the Constructors' Championship because there were no

It was with great difficulty that everyone had to accept that the championship was over

Benettons left on the track (Johnny Herbert had retired early) and there was a good prospect of a win for Nigel. The whole team deserved a medal of some sort for the way they had coped with the season. To win the Constructors' Championship and the race would help make the long job of dismantling and repacking more bearable. The thing that hurt, though, was not winning the drivers' title. But the race was something going on in the background as far as I was concerned.

I went back to the debrief room and got on the phone to Georgie. I said something like: 'I'm coming home. We'll just have to wait for another time.' She was suitably angry about what she felt had happened.

The reality was that I felt I had done the right thing the whole way through. There are occasions when a driver tries something, takes a chance, and it doesn't come off. He then blames himself for what happens. I did not feel that way. I had done the only thing possible because I had to take the opportunity when it arose.

On reflection, I could see from the replays of Michael's original accident that he would not have been able to continue in any case. He had actually hit the wall very hard. His right-rear wheel was out of alignment and he had probably smashed his suspension or punctured a tyre. He was out of the race from the moment he hit the wall. But I didn't know that. I got some satisfaction from the knowledge that I had given him a good race and pressured him into making a mistake. But he had always been the favourite, thanks to his one-point advantage. I had no alternative but to accept the facts.

'I'M COMING HOME.'
I SHARE THE BAD NEWS WITH
GEORGIE NOT LONG AFTER MY
RACE HAD ENDED

After the race, Michael made some remarks to the effect that he was retracting his criticism of me, made earlier in the season. I thought that was a little disingenuous because it was easy to say such things after he had won the championship. In actual fact, I saw him at breakfast the morning after the race. I congratulated him and said it must feel great. He said, yes, he felt terrific. He also said he wanted to apologize because he actually had a lot more respect for me now than he had felt before and he wished he hadn't said those things. Unfortunately, the respect of Michael Schumacher is no substitute for the world crown.

I told him that, next time, maybe he should be more careful before coming out with comments about his rivals. I wished him all the best and good luck for 1995, when we would both share Renault horsepower, albeit in different chassis. I don't know for sure, but I had the feeling that he was ever so slightly uncomfortable about my presence.

A RARE PLEASURE IS
GETTING AWAY FROM IT ALL
ON MY DUCATI

At last it was time to go home. I wanted very much to be back with the boys and Georgie whom I had not seen for over two weeks, which seemed a lifetime ago. In fact, since we had moved to the new house back in July I'd hardly spent any time there at all. But there was just the small matter of a twenty-two-hour flight and a 5 a.m. press conference immediately I arrived at Heathrow before the season would be truly over. Sure enough the questioning was heavily weighted in an attempt to get me to condemn Schumacher's driving and also to draw me on my plans for 1995. Would I be driving for Williams? Was Frank going to cough up? Is Schumacher a dirty rat? I did not have to say anything specific and in all honesty was hardly capable of thinking at all after so long without proper sleep (I had been up until 4.30 a.m. the night after the race and with more than one beer inside me!).

The climax to the season had been sensational. From such a tragic start, the sport had in many ways been reborn and no one would have celebrated that more than Roland and Ayrton. I felt many times during the year that to honour those guys and to show them the right sort of respect, the best thing that any driver could do was to accept the challenge of driving in Formula One with everything he had and to enjoy every second he could. I could truthfully say these things about myself and this went a long way to alleviating any disappointment I felt about not winning the championship.

When I started this book, there were two things on my mind. I was new to the sport and I wanted to comment on things before they became routine, things which would eventually be lost through familiarity. The other reason for writing the book was that I knew I was about to partner Ayrton Senna. That was going to be of particular interest since it would be a very rare privilege to work with such a great driver and compete against him. Sadly, that was not to be.

No one could have predicted the events of this season. Unpredictability is one of the most appealing things about the life of a racing driver and, indeed, of Formula One itself. People may say the sport follows a set pattern. But it doesn't. Tragedy or triumph, every season has a pattern which is unique and 1994 has been no exception. My hope is that this book, through the special skills of Jon Nicholson and my description and attempts to be as honest as possible, has given a valuable account of the life of a Formula One driver, not only for the true enthusiast but for anyone who cares to know. Drive carefully.

AT THE END OF A SEASON
FILLED WITH EVERY EMOTION,
I COULDN'T WAIT TO GET BACK
TO MY FAMILY

'It's the way I tell it, Damon.' The words in this book are entirely Damon's. I merely helped to arrange the story of an incredible season involving a remarkably honest and frequently underrated driver. Maurice Hamilton

This must be the first time he has laughed at one of my jokes in the last ten years! Our long-standing friendship took on a completely new dimension as I saw, at first hand, how Damon coped with the immense pressures and the way he rose above them to get the results the team so badly needed. Many thanks to all. Jon Nicholson

I would like to thank my publishers Macmillan, Williams Grand Prix Engineering, Renault, Rothmans Racing and Maurice Hamilton for their help in making this book possible.
Damon Hill. November 1994

First published 1994 by Macmillan London
an imprint of Macmillan General Books
Cavaye Place London SW10 9PG
Associated companies throughout the world

ISBN 0-333-62308-8 (HARDBACK)
ISBN 0-330-33781-5 (PAPERBACK)

Copyright text © Damon Hill 1994
Copyright photographs © Jon Nicholson 1994

The right of Damon Hill to be identified as the author of this work has been asserted by him in accordance with the Copyright, Designs and Patents Act 1988.

The right of Jon Nicholson to be identified as the photographer whose original photographs appear in this book has been asserted by him in accordance with the Copyright, Designs and Patents Act 1988.

All rights reserved. No reproduction, copy or transmission of this publication may be made without written permission. No paragraph may be reproduced, copied or transmitted save with the written permission or in accordance with the provisions of the Copyright Act 1956 (as amended). Any person who does any unauthorized act in relation to this publication may be liable to criminal prosecution and civil claims for damages.

9 8 7 6 5 4 3 2 1

A CIP catalogue record for this book is available from the British Library.

Designed and typeset by Macmillan General Books.

Colour reproduction by Aylesbury Studios, Bromley, Kent.

Printed and bound in Great Britain by BPC Hazell Ltd. A member of The British Printing Company Limited.

This book is sold subject to the condition that it shall not, by way of trade or otherwise, be lent, re-sold, hired out, or otherwise circulated without the publishers prior consent in any form of binding or cover other than that in which it is published and without a similar condition being imposed on the subsequent purchaser.